GENERATIONAL WEALTH & REAL ESTATE PLAYBOOK

GENERATIONAL WEALTH & REAL ESTATE PLAYBOOK

A PRACTICAL GUIDE TO BUILDING ASSETS, MINIMIZING TAXES, AND PROTECTING WEALTH FOR GENERATIONS

GLENN POLANSKY

Glenn Polansky
Generational Wealth & Real Estate Playbook

Disclaimer: The information in this book is for educational and informational purposes only and is based on the author's personal experiences. It is not intended as financial, legal, tax, or investment advice. Real estate investing involves risks, including loss of principal, and past performance is no guarantee of future results. Readers should consult with qualified professionals, such as financial advisors, attorneys, accountants, and tax experts, before making any decisions or implementing strategies discussed herein. The author and publisher disclaim any liability for actions taken based on this book's content. Laws and regulations vary by jurisdiction and change over time; always verify current rules applicable to your situation.

Printed in The United States of America
Published by Spines
ISBN:979-8-90223-285-8

Spines

This is for the younger generation who want a better starting line—who want to understand money, build assets early, and avoid the mistakes most people don't realize they're making until it's too late.

And it's for the parents who lie awake at night worrying about their children's future.

For those who believe there is a smarter path than living paycheck to paycheck and hoping things work out.

May these pages give you the confidence to act, the discipline to stay the course, and the belief that generational wealth is not reserved for the privileged few — but achievable for anyone willing to learn, commit, and lead their family forward.

This is your invitation to build not just income, but a legacy.

CONTENTS

ACKNOWLEDGMENTS

This book would not have been possible without the incredible support system surrounding me. I cannot thank my family enough for the countless hours spent reviewing drafts, scrubbing through chapters, reliving stories, and helping bring these pages to life. Your time, honesty, and commitment made this book stronger in every way.

To my amazing wife, **Theresa** — thank you for your unwavering love, patience, and belief in me. You have always been a true team player. As we built this portfolio of wealth for ourselves and for our children, we did it together — side by side through every challenge and every win. I appreciate you more than words can express.

To my incredible children, **Tyler, Jordan, and Ryan** — you are the reason this journey began. If it weren't for each of you being born, none of this would have happened. You are my daily inspiration, my motivation, and my constant reminder to be better — not just as a provider, but as a father and leader. Everything I build is for you and for the generations that will follow.

I also want to thank my parents, my entire family, and my close friends who read this book multiple times, offering thoughtful feedback, insight, and encouragement. Your suggestions helped shape this book into what it is today.

To all of you — thank you for believing in this vision, for supporting me throughout this journey, and for being such a meaningful part of my foundation. This book carries all of you within its pages.

"Nothing in this world can take the place of persistence.

Talent will not; nothing is more common than unsuccessful men with talent.

Genius will not; unrewarded genius is almost a proverb.

Education will not; the world is full of educated derelicts.

Persistence and determination alone are omnipotent."

CALVIN COOLIDGE

"I do not think there is any other quality so essential to success of any kind as the quality of perseverance."

JOHN D. ROCKEFELLER

"The goal is not to be rich for a moment, but to be secure for generations."

LEGACY WEALTH PHILOSOPHY

A $100,000 OPPORTUNITY IS HIDDEN INSIDE THIS BOOK

THE GENERATIONAL WEALTH CHALLENGE

What if reading this book could help change your family's financial future?

For generations, the strategies used to build wealth through real estate, tax planning, and asset protection have been quietly passed down among a small group of people.

This book was written to open that knowledge to everyone.

But we wanted to do something even more powerful.

We wanted to **turn education into opportunity.**

So we created **The Generational Wealth Challenge.**

Through this program, **The Guide To Wealth, LLC will award ten (10) grants valued at $100,000 each** to help individuals take their first step into income-producing real estate.

Each grant is designed to help a winner acquire their **first 2–4 family property** — the same type of investment that has helped many families build long-term generational wealth.

Each grant package includes:

- **$70,000 toward a property down payment**

- **Legal support for entity formation and asset protection**
- **Tax strategy planning and structuring**
- **Coaching and deal guidance from experienced real estate professionals**

But here's where things get interesting.

Your entry to the Challenge is hidden inside this book.

Throughout the pages of this book you will find **nine small graphics**.

Hidden inside each graphic is **one letter**.

Those **nine letters combine to form a two-word catch phrase.**

Your challenge is to **find each letter and piece together the phrase.**

Once you uncover the phrase, you can submit it to enter **The Generational Wealth Challenge**.

READY TO START THE HUNT?

As you read through the book, keep your eyes open for the hidden graphics.

Each one contains **one letter of the phrase.**

Find all nine letters…

Put the phrase together…

And you may unlock your chance to win a **$100,000 Generational Wealth Grant.**

When you find the phrase

Visit: **theguidetowealth.com**

Submit the phrase along with your proof of purchase to enter the Challenge.

You can also learn how to earn **additional entries** and increase your chances of being selected.

Full details of the Challenge, official rules, and entry instructions can be found in the **Generational Wealth Challenge section at the end of this book.**

One book.

Nine hidden letters.

A chance to build Legacy Now.

Your search begins on the next page.

INTRODUCTION

The title of this book is no gimmick. It's what I wish someone had handed me at twenty-two. A roadmap. A wake-up call. A push to stop making excuses and just start.

If I really had access to Doc Emmett Brown's DeLorean from *Back to the Future,* I wouldn't waste it picking lottery numbers or warning myself about the 2008 stock market crash. I'd gun it to 88 mph, land right in front of my 22-year-old self, swing open those gullwing doors and step out holding this book. Doc would be right there yelling, "Great Scott!" while I handed it over and said, "Listen—stop making excuses. Act now! Don't wait for perfect, because perfect never comes." It's fun to imagine the smoke, sparks, and flux capacitor glowing in the background, but the truth is, you don't need a time machine to change your future. You just need the guts to start today. Since I can't go back, I'm writing this for you. Don't just read it. Use it. Take one step today that gets you closer to financial freedom.

That is why I decided to write this book. This isn't a book of abstract theories, recycled formulas, or motivational slogans. It's the raw, lived experience of someone who started from scratch, made costly errors, but eventually uncovered the timeless principles that build wealth. It's the same playbook I want my kids—and now you—to follow so you can accelerate your journey.

First, I need you to understand something: this has been a long journey for me. From as far back as I can remember, I carried an entrepreneurial spirit and a competitive drive that pushed me to always want more. By the time I was ten, tennis had become the sport that tested me both mentally and physically. My parents had a simple philosophy: *if you want something badly enough, work for it.*

Every journey has a moment when abstraction becomes real.

For me, it happened in Red Bank, New Jersey.

I'll never forget that drive down the Garden State Parkway. The wagon rattled as I pushed it past sixty miles per hour and, of course, closer to seventy-five. When I finally pulled into Red Bank, I couldn't help but notice the difference. The streets were lined with trees, the houses bigger, the lawns perfectly kept. The whole place seemed to hum with success.

At the house, nobody answered the front door, but I heard voices out back. I walked around and froze. Behind the gate sat a massive yacht, gleaming in the sun. My jaw dropped. In that moment, I wasn't thinking about the boat motor anymore. I was mesmerized by the boat.

The owner walked over with a smile and said something that rewired my brain.

"This boat was free."

"Free? What do you mean?" I asked.

"Fifteen years ago, I bought my first multi-family house. My tenants paid the mortgage. Eventually, I refinanced, pulled the equity out tax-free, and bought this boat," he explained.

It was like the universe handed me a secret formula: wealth isn't about luck or inheritance. It's about assets. It was about the system:

- Buy assets
- Use leverage responsibly
- Let tenants pay down debt
- Recycle equity
- Repeat

No brilliance required. Just discipline and time.

Wealth isn't about luck or inheritance. It's about assets.

That moment lit the fire. And I'll be honest—it haunted me for years. I knew exactly what I needed to do, but I hesitated. I second-guessed. I squandered time I could have been building wealth. That regret became its own lesson:

Don't procrastinate. Don't overthink. Don't wait for the "perfect time." If you put in the effort and take the risk, it will pay off.

I couldn't shake it. That night, as I lay in bed, the word free kept echoing in my head. Could something as massive as a yacht really be free if tenants paid for it? The answer was yes—and that realization consumed me.

I devoured books like Think and Grow Rich and Rich Dad Poor Dad. I scribbled notes, underlined passages, and pestered anyone who seemed to know even a little about real estate. At the time, my wife and I were living in a roach-infested apartment in California, scraping by on tight budgets, but every sacrifice felt like another brick laid toward freedom.

Friends were buying new cars and clothes. We were buying time and discipline. Every dollar had a purpose. Every sacrifice had a timeline. I repeated one phrase constantly: Without dreams, there are no goals. Without goals, there is no future.

Years later, back in New Jersey, I finally got my first big bonus. Many people would have spent it on a car, a trip, or paying down bills. For me, it was a test: consume or invest?

Without dreams, there are no goals. Without goals, there is no future.

I remembered the man in Red Bank and his tenants paying his mortgage. I knew what I had to do. That bonus didn't represent money. It represented possibility. It was my first seed of financial freedom.

This book is the roadmap, a guide not of shortcuts but of systems. Systems that work for ordinary people who want extraordinary results.

If you've ever felt trapped in the grind, tired of trading time for money, or stuck wondering how others seem to "figure it out" while you spin your wheels, this book is for you.

My promise is simple: I'll explain the principles clearly, define every term, and share my missteps as openly as my wins. Financial freedom isn't just about money. It's about time, choices, and independence.

With these foundational principles in mind, let's dive into the practical steps that turned my vision into reality, starting with the very first deal.

Turn the page. Your roadmap begins here.

CHAPTER 1
FOUNDATIONS & MINDSET

A LETTER TO MY YOUNGER SELF

Dear Younger Me,

I'm writing this from the other side of experience—the side where patterns finally make sense, where mistakes reveal their lessons, and where time proves to be either your greatest ally or your most expensive enemy.

If I could go back and hand you something, it wouldn't be advice scribbled on a napkin or a motivational quote. It would be this book. Not because it contains secrets, but because it contains clarity—the kind you only earn after years of trial, hesitation, and finally, action.

I wouldn't warn you about market crashes or whisper stock tips. I wouldn't tell you to avoid failure. Failure is necessary. What I would tell you is this:

- Stop waiting for certainty.
- Stop confusing preparation with progress.
- And stop assuming you have more time than you do.

Most people don't fail financially because they make terrible decisions. They fail because they make no decision—year after year—while life quietly locks in their future.

This book exists because I learned too late that no one is coming to rescue you financially. Schools don't teach this. Employers don't reward it. And society often discourages it. Financial freedom is a path you have to choose deliberately—and early.

Before we talk about real estate, numbers, or systems, we need to talk about something far more important: how you think. Because mindset determines behavior, and behavior determines outcomes.

If you get this part wrong, nothing else works.

Your Older Self

THE MINDSET OF WEALTH BUILDING

My financial foundation was laid long before I ever bought my first investment property. It didn't start with money; it started with discipline.

I was finally starting to find my way. The nervous excitement of those first closings—the shaky hands, the race to wire funds before the bank cut-off—had faded into something deeper and steadier. I was beginning to understand that if I was going to win this game long-term, I couldn't just work for money. Money had to start working for me.

That idea sounds like a motivational poster on a breakroom wall until you've lived it. When you're young—when the rent is due, the car needs tires, and the kids need shoes—passive income feels like a fairy tale. At that stage, I was still a W-2 earner. I had structure, a salary, and the illusion of security. But the more I looked at my life—and at the lives of people twenty years ahead of me—the clearer it became: the paycheck alone wasn't going to buy freedom. If I wanted to be free by fifty, every dollar had to be put on assignment. Every dollar needed a job that outlived me.

Before real estate became my primary focus, I bought and sold companies, making millions in the process. But that success came at a price. The stress was constant. Day in and day out, I was in the trenches—transforming businesses, making payroll, hiring and firing, managing cash flow, and carrying the weight of every decision. It was the full nine yards, and there were many days it felt overwhelming.

That chapter of my life gave me something far more valuable than money: *skills*. The ability to read numbers, make decisions under pressure, manage risk, solve problems, and keep moving forward when quitting would've been easier. Those skills became the backbone of everything I later did in real estate—and they're transferable to any business, any market, and any economic cycle.

But what truly changed my course—what forced me to stop and reassess everything—was **time**.

One of my closest friends, Andrew, passed away suddenly from a heart attack. I was devastated. Then, within weeks, my fraternity brother and college roommate Garth from Rutgers died from a heart condition. Two losses. Back-to-back. No warning. That was it.

In that moment, I realized something that no balance sheet or deal ever taught me: it was time. No amount of money, success, or hustle can negotiate with it. And I asked myself a hard question—why was I trading my most valuable years for stress, while telling myself I'd "enjoy life later"?

I also thought about my kids. I didn't want them growing up with economic anxiety. I didn't want them watching their father grind endlessly, only to be too exhausted to live. I wanted them to see what control looks like—not just financial control, but control over time, choices, and life itself. So I reshaped everything.

I sold my medical group practice. I doubled down on real estate. I restructured my portfolio, my priorities, and my pace. I shifted from building businesses that consumed me to building assets that worked for me. And in doing so, I took my real estate portfolio to an entirely new level—one built not just for income, but for freedom and longevity.

Today, I enjoy every minute of it. I'm present. I'm building something that will outlive me. And I'm creating a portfolio designed not just to support my life, but also generations to come.

Money can be lost and rebuilt. Assets can come and go. But skills, discipline, and perspective last forever. That's what I'm passing on to you. Because if I lost everything tomorrow, I know I could rebuild it again. That confidence doesn't come from money in the bank—it comes from knowing how the game works and choosing to play it on your terms.

"LESSON: TIME IS THE ULTIMATE ASSET"

As a kid, I picked up a paper route and made $36 a week. That money bought me one private tennis lesson for $32, leaving me just $4 left-over. It wasn't glamorous. It was cold, repetitive, and invisible. But it taught me something early: if I wanted anything beyond the basics, I had to earn it. No shortcuts. No excuses.

From the paper route, I moved on to working at a tennis club, cleaning courts and locker rooms—whatever it took to make a few extra dollars. The best part? If a court was open, I could practice. And I did, every chance I got. Over time, my commitment grew. I wasn't just hitting balls anymore. I was training every day with the dream of becoming a professional tennis player.

To fund that dream, I went from cleaning courts to waiting tables and eventually bartending, pouring nearly everything I earned into coaches, trainers, and travel. Those sacrifices paid off: I was recruited to play Division I tennis at Rutgers. I redshirted my first year due to poor grades, but I kept pushing forward. When my personal coach encouraged me to leave and hit the professional circuit, I didn't feel ready. The truth is, no athlete ever really feels ready. You just compete, adapt, and keep going. Looking back, I'm grateful he pushed me.

My father, however, was not so pleased. He made me promise him I'd finish my degree. So I compromised. I loaded up on easy classes, returned to campus only for midterms and finals, and kept my focus on tennis. It wasn't glamorous, but it allowed me to do both. In the end, I barely graduated, but I kept my word to him.

I played tournaments, landed a sponsorship with Mizuno Sports, and spent three years grinding it out on the circuit. But with debt piling up, I had to face reality: I wasn't going to reach the level I had dreamed of. Walking away was tough, but what I gained was invaluable. I learned how to survive on my own, how to travel the world, and most importantly, that success requires discipline without anyone standing over your shoulder. No one tells you to get up at 6 a.m. to train. No one forces you to eat right or to keep practicing when you're exhausted. You either do it or you don't.

"Discipline in one area of life becomes the fuel for success in every area."

That same persistence, drive, and determination never left me. Today, I apply it to business and real estate in the exact same way I once applied it to tennis. And that's what this book is about. Building wealth isn't a "get rich quick" scheme. It's a roadmap. It's about showing up, grinding, and staying the course. And one day you'll look back and realize the drive was worth it because your kids and grandkids will thank you for laying the foundation of generational wealth.

After tennis, I took a job as the head tennis coach for a college in New Jersey. I even started my own tennis academy in the summers and worked with some great kids along the way. Soon, I realized this wasn't what I wanted long-term. That's when my Uncle Al stepped in. He was my mentor, one of my best friends, and a guiding force who encouraged me to pursue a career in health-care administration. I admired him deeply. He was sharp, thoughtful, and I hung on every word of advice he gave me.

With his encouragement, I decided to aim high and apply to a top graduate program in health-care administration. Around that time, I also met my future wife at a tennis club where I was teaching part-time. Life was beginning to shift. My uncle, who taught as an adjunct professor at Berkeley, wanted to help me get into the right program. But there was one problem: my undergrad grades were horrendous. I had focused everything on tennis and left academics behind.

I knew I had to prove myself, so I hired a tutor and a strategist to help me prepare for the Graduate Management Admission Test. I aced it, scoring high enough to get noticed. My uncle encouraged me to head to California, where I secured an in-person interview with USC. They understood that my life had been consumed by tennis, and while my grades didn't reflect my potential, my test score proved I had the ability. They took a chance on me, admitting me on academic probation.

That chance changed everything. I committed to working harder than ever. With the support of my fiancée—who later became my wife—I pushed myself, determined to succeed. Not only did I graduate, but I also earned my master's in health administration with honors.

From there, I launched into a career that took me through some of the top names in health care: Ernst & Young, Sutter Health, Columbia and Cornell, and Aetna, just to name a few. It wasn't always easy, and for years, I was still trying to figure out exactly where I fit. But I stayed the course and built financial stability. Later, when real estate entered my life, I realized something surprising: the skill set transfers. Investing rewards consistency far more than brilliance. It punishes entitlement and excuses ruthlessly.

Another foundational pillar was family. My wife, Theresa, believed in the long game before it paid off. We lived modestly—not because we had to, but because we chose to. While others upgraded cars and vacations, we upgraded patience.

Our children became my why. I wasn't just trying to build wealth; I was trying to build options. Options for education. Options for freedom. Options for a life not constrained by paycheck dependency.

One of the hardest mindset shifts I had to make was letting go of the employee identity. Employees are trained to trade time for money and seek approval for progress. Investors build systems that function without their constant presence.

Fear plays a role here. Fear of debt. Fear of mistakes. Fear of being judged. But fear doesn't vanish with more information; it vanishes with action.

Confidence is not the absence of fear. It's the result of repeated exposure.

Lifestyle discipline matters more than income. I've seen high earners sabotage themselves with lifestyle inflation. I chose a different path: assets first, rewards later.

Credit became another pillar. Your credit score isn't a number—it's your financial reputation. Lenders don't care how smart you are; they care how reliable you've been. Missed payments close doors quietly. Strong credit opens them silently.

Treat credit like a business partner—because that's exactly what it becomes.

UNDERSTANDING MONEY

Once your mindset shifts, your understanding of money has to shift with it. Most people are taught a very narrow financial script: earn money, save money, and avoid debt at all costs. Almost no one is taught how money actually behaves or how wealth is truly built over time.

Unfortunately, I didn't fully grasp this until much later in life. Two critical concepts were missing from my early financial education—and they changed everything once I understood them: the power of compounding and the intelligent use of leverage. These are not secrets, but they are rarely taught to the masses. Wealthy families understand them, teach them early, and build their entire financial strategies around them.

Compounding rewards patience and consistency. Leverage, when used responsibly, accelerates growth by allowing your money to work harder than you ever could on your own. Together, these two forces are the foundation of real wealth creation. Remember this. Learn it. Respect it. And most importantly, use it intentionally.

The distinction between assets and liabilities changed everything for me. An asset puts money in your pocket. A liability takes money out. This sounds simple, but it explains why so many financially responsible people remain stuck. They earn well, save diligently, and then spend their surplus on liabilities disguised as rewards.

Debt operates the same way. Bad debt funds consumption. Good debt funds assets. But there's a third category I didn't understand for years: great debt—fixed-rate, long-term debt attached to income-producing assets.

Inflation quietly punishes savers. Money sitting still loses purchasing power every year. Saving feels safe, but safety can be deceptive.

I learned this firsthand during my corporate career. I worked for respected organizations. I helped build successful platforms. Then one day, in a polished boardroom, the decision was made to shut everything down.

Years of effort disappeared instantly. That was the day I fully understood this truth: A paycheck is not security. Assets are. Real estate appealed to me because it compounds in multiple dimensions simultaneously:

- Appreciation
- Loan paydown

- Cash flow
- Tax advantages

All while someone else—the tenant—services the debt. This is why real estate behaves differently from traditional investments. It's not linear. It's layered.

People often ask, "How many properties do I need to retire?" The question itself reveals a misunderstanding. Retirement isn't about property count; it's about income replacement.

The formula is straightforward:

Annual Expenses ÷ Reliable Cash Flow = Freedom Number

Once you see it this way, financial independence becomes a math problem, not a mystery.

Money, ultimately, is a tool. Used intentionally, it buys time, choice, and peace of mind. Used carelessly, it buys stress and fragility. I was after, and what we all want is relief from financial stress, and what I realized is that wealth with assets is the absence of economic anxiety.

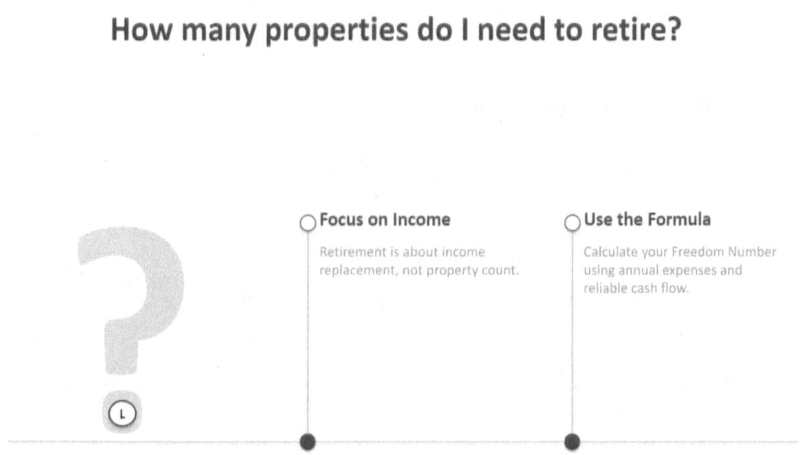

The math is simpler than most people think. It comes down to three variables:

E – Your annual personal expenses (the amount you need each year to live and save for retirement).

R – The average annual *net* cash-on-cash return from your rental properties (your after-expense cash flow expressed as a percentage of the cash you invested).

W – The total equity or wealth you must build in real estate to meet those expenses.

The formula is:

$$\mathbf{E \div R = W}$$

That tells you the total *equity* you need to generate enough cash flow to cover your lifestyle.

Step-by-Step Example

Let's run a real scenario.

Assumptions

Annual living expenses (**E**): $90,000

Target cash-on-cash return (**R**): 8% (0.08 as a decimal)

Plug the numbers in:

$$\mathbf{W = 90{,}000 \div 0.08 = \$1{,}125{,}000}$$

So, you need about $1.13 million in equity producing an 8% net return to cover a $90,000 lifestyle.

Translating Equity into Doors

If you average $250/month in *net* cash flow per door (after all expenses, reserves, and property management):

$$\$90{,}000 \div (\$250 \times 12) \approx 30 \text{ units.}$$

That's thirty well-run units, not 30 buildings. You could reach this with:

- Ten triplexes,
- Five six-unit properties,
- Or a mix of 2- to 4-families.

The key is the *net* cash flow, not the number of doors. Higher cash-flowing markets or better financing could cut that number in half.

A Real-Life Illustration

Let's call him **Daniel**, followed this roadmap.

He bought his first duplex at 28, adding one small multifamily a year for six years. By 35, he owned 14 units with an average net cash flow of $325 per door. His math:

$$14 \text{ units} \times \$325 \times 12 = \$54{,}600 \text{ net annual income.}$$

That covered his modest $50,000 living expenses, giving him financial independence—*before* his peers even maxed out their 401(k)s.

Daniel still works because he enjoys it, but he no longer *has* to. That's the power of knowing your number.

Key Takeaways

Know E – Track every expense until you have a real annual figure.

Target R – Focus on realistic cash-on-cash returns (6–10% is a solid goal).

Scale to W – Use the formula E ÷ R to find your equity target, then buy enough doors to hit the cash flow that supports your life.

When you can say, *"My properties pay my bills whether I work or not,"* you've reached financial freedom—*and* you know exactly how many rentals it took to get there.

Now that we've covered the mindset shift and basic math for financial freedom, let's contrast the limitations of traditional saving with the power of strategic investing. I live by the Five Ps: Proper Planning Prevents Poor Performance.

THE BASICS THAT CHANGED EVERYTHING

Before my first purchase, I committed to deeply learning the fundamentals. Let's pause here and define a few of the words that became the cornerstone of my journey:

- Asset: Something that puts money in your pocket. A rental property is an asset because tenants pay you rent every month.
- Liability: Something that takes money out of your pocket. That yacht? A liability. It doesn't generate income. It drains it.

- Debt: Money borrowed with the obligation to pay it back. Most people fear debt, but smart debt, such as debt used to buy income-producing assets, is one of the fastest wealth-builders there is.
- Cap Rate (Capitalization Rate): A simple way to measure the return on a property, it is calculated as Net Operating Income ÷ Purchase Price. For example, if a property earns $60,000 a year and costs $1,000,000, the cap rate is 6%. The higher the cap rate, the better your return.
- Leverage: Using borrowed money (like a mortgage) to amplify returns.
- Compound Interest: Earning interest on interest—great when rates are high, weak when they're low.
- Opportunity Cost: The loss of potential gain when you choose one option over another (like saving vs. investing).

Once I understood those terms, I realized that the man in Red Bank had unlocked the formula: buy assets that pay you, use debt wisely, and let time multiply the results. These concepts became filters. They removed emotion and replaced it with clarity. I learned quickly that discipline isn't restrictive—it's freeing. When rules are clear, decisions become easy.

Traditional paths promise safety. In reality, they promise predictability—until they don't.

I watched capable people lose jobs through no fault of their own. I watched entire departments disappear. Loyalty didn't protect them.

That's when I stopped outsourcing my future to any institution.

Ownership changes everything.

Assets first. Lifestyle later

ASSETS FIRST, LIFESTYLE LATER

This became my operating rule:

Assets first. Lifestyle later.

Not never—later.

This isn't deprivation. It's sequencing.

People who reverse the order stay busy forever. People who delay gratification briefly buy freedom permanently.

THE QUIET REWARD

The best part wasn't the vacations or the nice car. It was the ability to finally be financially free. I no longer had to depend on corporate America, worry about losing a job, or live in fear that I couldn't pay the mortgage, put food on the table, or buy clothes for my family. That constant stress—the weight so many people carry—was gone. After years of grinding, I had achieved my goal. My dream.

And here's the thing most people don't realize: freedom isn't about money—it's about options. When you have assets working for you, your income no longer comes with strings attached. You don't wake up dreading the alarm clock because you're chained to a paycheck. Instead, you get to wake up with a sense of control. You choose how to spend your day, who you spend it with, and what you work on. That's the true reward of building assets and adopting the right mindset: choice.

Freedom also means resilience. When the economy dips, when layoffs happen, when markets shift, the average person panics. But when you've built a foundation of assets, you have stability. Your properties still produce income, your systems still work, and you still sleep at night. That peace of mind is worth more than any luxury car or fancy watch.

And let me be clear: this wasn't an overnight success story. It took years of persistence, sacrifice, and discipline to get here. But once I crossed the line from survival to freedom, I realized the quiet reward wasn't just for me—it was for my family, and for the generations to come. My kids won't grow up with the same financial fear I once had. They'll grow up with a roadmap.

That's why I say building wealth through real estate isn't just about money—it's about rewriting your story. It's about creating a life where stress no longer controls you, and where opportunity becomes your default setting.

COMPOUNDING, LEVERAGE, AND YOUR FREEDOM NUMBER

The first time rent covered a mortgage, the theory became tangible. Equity grew quietly. Cash flow appeared monthly. Options multiplied.

This is compounding in real life—not on a statement, but in lived experience.

Your freedom number isn't abstract. It's personal. And it's achievable far sooner than most people think—if they start early.

CONCLUSION

Mindset doesn't replace action—it enables it.

In the next chapter, we move from foundation to execution: the first deal, the first numbers, the first leap that turns intention into momentum.

CHAPTER 2
STARTING YOUR REAL ESTATE JOURNEY

GETTING INTO THE GAME: YOUR FIRST PROPERTY

There comes a moment when preparation quietly turns into procrastination. I reached that moment without realizing it at first.

I had read the books. I understood the theory. I could explain leverage, cash flow, and appreciation to anyone who asked. But I didn't own a property. Knowledge without ownership creates a false sense of progress—it feels productive, but nothing changes.

The catalyst was a bonus check from my W-2 job. With my first bonus check in hand, I felt both exhilarated and terrified. For years, I had dreamed of breaking free from the cycle of working hard, saving money, and watching that money grow at a snail's pace in a bank account. Now, finally, I had a lump sum that could be the seed for something bigger.

My wife and I sat at the kitchen table late one evening, the check still crisp in my hands. We were both nervous. We didn't know anything about being landlords, and we had no family members or mentors to guide us. All we had was a shared determination to try.

"I don't know," she said, her voice betraying both caution and curiosity. "What if it's a disaster? What if tenants don't pay? What if it's more stress than we can handle?"

I shrugged, but my heart was pounding. "If we buy it right," I said, "and it doesn't work out, then we just sell it and move on. But if it does work."

She looked at me, half smiling, and said, "Then maybe it's the start of something."

That was all I needed: Permission. Partnership. A green light to take the leap.

It wasn't life-changing money, but it was enough to force a decision. I could spend it, save it, or deploy it.

I chose deployment.

At the same time, my wife and I were thinking long-term. College tuition was rising faster than wages. Saving felt responsible, but it didn't feel sufficient. I needed an asset that could:

- Outpace inflation
- Produce income
- Grow without constant oversight

That's when I committed to multi-family real estate.

Single-family rentals can work, but they magnify early risk. One vacancy means zero income. Multi-family properties spread risk immediately. Even with one vacant unit, income continues.

More importantly, multi-family properties teach faster. You learn tenant management, maintenance, and cash flow dynamics all at once.

My goal wasn't appreciation or tax strategy. It was simpler and more disciplined:

Buy income-producing property that pays me while I learn.

BUILDING YOUR INVESTMENT RULES (YOUR EARLY SYSTEM)

Vision alone wasn't enough. I needed a system to keep me from making emotional decisions.

I didn't want to get caught up in pretty kitchens, fresh paint, or an agent's sales pitch, so I built what I called my *Financial Real Estate*

Analyzer. At first, it was just a crude Excel spreadsheet, but to me it was revolutionary.

I spent late nights teaching myself formulas, researching what professional investors used, and plugging in numbers until I had something that could tell me—in black and white—whether a deal was worth it.

Here's what it tracked:

1

Metric	Formula or Requirement
Monthly Cash Flow	Gross Rent – Operating Expenses – Mortgage Payment
Net Operating Income (NOI)	Gross Operating Income (GOI) – Operating Expenses
Cap Rate (Capitalization Rate)	Net Operating Income ÷ Purchase Price
Cash-on-Cash Return	Annual Cash Flow[1] ÷ Cash Invested
15-Year Equity Paydown	Equity Paydown = Loan Amount – Remaining Loan Balance After 15 Years
Debt Service Coverage Ratio (DSCR)	NOI ÷ Debt Payments
Vacancy	I used a standard industry factor of 3% in NJ, but it should be adjusted by county/by state. This is what the large institutional banks use; in reality, where I am, my vacancy factor is hours.
T-12 Scrub	Short for trailing 12-month detail of all income and expenses — e.g., all gas, electric, water, pest control, etc.
Structural Reserves	Typically, I use a factor of $200 a unit per year, but adjust based on my assessment of the units after any inspections.

1. Note: Annual Cash Flow is the total net income a property generates over the course of a year after all expenses and debt payments are deducted from rental income. It's essentially the money that's left in your pocket at the end of the year, and it's a key measure of an investment property's profitability.

Monthly Cash Flow: *Gross Rent – Operating Expenses – Mortgage Payment*

If it wasn't positive, I didn't buy.

Cap Rate (Capitalization Rate): *Net Operating Income ÷ Purchase Price*

I set a minimum threshold. If it didn't hit that number, I passed, at first my threshold was at least 1% over the mortgage rate.

Cash-on-Cash Return: *Annual Cash Flow*[2] *÷ Cash Invested*

This told me how hard my actual dollars were working.

15-Year Equity Paydown: When I first imagined buying property, it wasn't about becoming wealthy or building an empire. My vision was simple: I wanted to buy one multi-family house, put a fifteen-year mortgage on it, and let time do the work.

My daughter was two years old at the time. By the time she went off to college, the mortgage would be paid off, and I'd be sitting on a free-and-clear property with built-up equity. I could refinance or sell it and, just like that, pay for her education.

That was my plan. Not glamorous. Not even "investing" in the way people talk about it today. It was just smart savings with leverage. Instead of putting money into a 529 plan and hoping the stock market cooperated, I wanted a tangible asset, one that generated cash flow along the way.

What I didn't realize was that this small, calculated decision would set the stage for a lifelong journey into real estate, tax strategies, and generational wealth.

DSCR (Debt Service Coverage Ratio):

---

2. Note: Annual Cash Flow is the total net income a property generates over the course of a year after all expenses and debt payments are deducted from rental income. It's essentially the money that's left in your pocket at the end of the year, and it's a key measure of an investment property's profitability.

NOI ÷ Debt Payments. Lenders want DSCR ≥ 1.25

Anything lower means the property might not pay its mortgage reliably.

Net Operating Income (NOI) is a key performance metric in real estate investing. It represents the income a property generates after operating expenses are deducted, but before financing costs, taxes, and depreciation are considered.

Gross Operating Income (GOI) is the total rental income plus any other income from the property (e.g., parking fees, laundry, storage), minus vacancy and credit loss.

Operating expenses are costs required to keep the property running: —property management, repairs, maintenance, insurance, utilities (if landlord-paid), and property taxes.

A T-12 stands for *Trailing 12 Months*. It's a report of all the income and expenses a property has generated over the past 12 months. Sellers and brokers often provide this to show the financial performance of a property. But here's the catch: what they hand you is usually filled with pro forma numbers—that is, projections or best-case scenarios. A T-12 Scrub is when you, as the investor, go line by line through that report and rebuild it yourself using actual numbers: bank statements, invoices, utility bills, repair receipts, etc. (you request this detail from the seller during due diligence).

It wasn't fancy. It wasn't Wall Street. But it gave me confidence. If it met all my rules, it gets my buy box.

My Buy-Box

- Cap Rate: ≥ 6–7%
- Cash-on-Cash: ≥ 8–12%
- DSCR: ≥ 1.25–1.35
- Rent-to-Price: ≥ 0.8–1.0%+
- Clear Value-Add Potential

If it doesn't hit all of these? I walk.

Emotion is the silent killer of first deals. You fall in love with finishes, layouts, or "potential." The Analyzer didn't care about potential. It cared about performance.

The rules were simple:

- Positive cash flow from day one
- Conservative expense assumptions
- Fixed-rate debt only
- Safe, livable neighborhoods
- No deals that required "perfect execution" to work

I learned quickly that discipline isn't restrictive—it's freeing. When rules are clear, decisions become easy. This system also protected me from my ego. I didn't need to win a deal. I needed the deal to win for me. And I learned early on that what works for me doesn't necessarily work for a partner.

WHY MULTI-FAMILY WAS THE SMARTEST FIRST STEP

I never wanted my first investment to be a single-family home, and here's why:

Single-family risk: With only one tenant, if that tenant pays late or stops paying altogether, you're carrying the entire mortgage yourself. In a multi-family property, the risk is spread out. For example, in a four-unit building, I only need income from roughly two and a half tenants to cover my mortgage and expenses.

More doors, more leverage: More units mean more potential for passive income and faster equity growth. Your money works smarter when it's producing rent from several doors, not just one.

Avoid HOAs, condos, or CDDs: Would not recommend buying a condo, townhome, or anything in a Community Development District (CDD) as an investment. You have zero control over HOA fees or special assessments. They can raise dues overnight and destroy your margins.

A friend of mine in Florida was doing great with a few condos until new legislation required massive reserve funds. His dues tripled almost overnight. He couldn't raise rents fast enough to cover the spike, property values dropped, and his cash flow vanished. Lesson learned: stay away from properties where someone else controls the expenses.

My Non-Negotiables (Written on the Wall)

Alongside the Analyzer, I wrote out strict investment rules and taped them to the wall above my desk. They looked like this:

Type of property: Multi-family, ideally two to four units.

Location: Within driving distance, in neighborhoods where rents were stable (I also like to keep it in close range so I can save money doing repairs myself and manage my properties).

Rent-to-Price Ratio: Monthly rent had to equal at least 1% of the purchase price.

Condition: Livable but with room for improvement. No gut rehabs.

Financing: Fixed-rate mortgage only. No gimmicks.

Cash Flow: Positive from day one—no exceptions.

If a property didn't meet those rules, I walked away. No matter how charming it looked. No matter how persuasive the agent was.

These criteria were my safety net. They gave me the confidence to act when others froze in fear.

Taking Action

Most people don't fail because they're incapable. They fail because they never start. They stay in the world of "someday" while time ticks by.

I've seen it too many times. I've got a buddy I've known for years. I kept encouraging him to invest—telling him about the deals I was finding, showing him how it was working for me. And every time, he had another excuse.

"I need more money."

"I'm busy with the kids."

My business isn't stable yet."

"I'll start after I finish building the deck."

Excuse after excuse after excuse. I call it **analysis paralysis**—always analyzing, never pulling the trigger. He spun in that cycle for twenty years. And now, he finally admits he wasted decades waiting for the perfect moment that never came. He's trying now, but time isn't on his side anymore.

That's why this chapter exists. If all you do is read this book and nod your head, nothing changes. If you actually take action, everything changes.

THE "TIME MACHINE" LESSON

If I could go back in time and hand a single book to my younger self, this would be the one. It took me decades—filled with sleepless nights, trial and error, and more mistakes than I'd like to admit—to uncover the principles of wealth creation. Lessons that now seem obvious once felt like mysteries. If I could walk up to that 22-year-old version of myself, place this roadmap in his hands, and whisper, *"Follow this path. Don't waste time. Don't repeat my mistakes"*—it would have changed everything.

PARTNERSHIP PITFALLS

On paper, partnerships make sense. More capital. Shared workload. Faster growth. In reality, partnerships introduce interpretation—and interpretation creates friction. I've seen deals stall because:

- Risk tolerance wasn't aligned
- Effort expectations differed
- Exit timelines weren't discussed
- Decision authority wasn't clear

Don't share control of long-term assets

One of my best friends watched me build my portfolio and said, *"Hey, let's do a deal together."*

It sounded harmless. We trusted each other. We thought it would be fun, profitable, and a way to share the ride. At first, it was great. We were excited, aligned, and optimistic. But over time, cracks appeared. I was doing most of the work—running the numbers, coordinating repairs, managing tenants, balancing the books. Yet at the end of the month, the split was still fifty-fifty.

That imbalance wore me down, and eventually it wore down the friendship. We didn't end with hugs and handshakes; we ended with tension, a buyout, and distance. Looking back, the deal wasn't worth the cost.

Years later, another friend wanted in. You'd think I'd have learned the first time. But like many entrepreneurs, I told myself, *This time it'll be different.*

Together, we bought an eighteen-unit building with a daycare center and another fifteen-unit building. Bigger deal, bigger upside. For two years, it worked. Then life changed for him. He wanted out. He wanted his cash back. Meanwhile, I wanted to hold. My strategy has always been long-term wealth, not quick flips.

We weren't aligned. And when partners aren't aligned, the deal can't survive.

A lot of folks dream about partnering with buddies, family members, people you play golf with or grab beers with. It sounds exciting at first. The promise of shared risk, shared workload, and shared wins sounds great. But what usually happens is stress, misalignment, and broken relationships. It almost never works long-term. I've tried it, I've seen others try it, and in almost every case, partnerships with friends or family collapse. Maybe not in the first six months. Maybe not even in the first year. But give it time. Life changes, priorities shift, money pressures mount, and suddenly that "dream team" becomes a nightmare. My advice: Don't do it.

Eventually, I adopted a simple rule: I don't share control of long-term assets. That doesn't mean I reject help. It means I structure involvement carefully. I prefer clean structures—fixed returns, documented terms, finite timelines. Freedom loves simplicity.

There's only one kind of partnership I trust—one where the vision, goals, and timeline are shared at the deepest level. For me, that's my wife, Theresa, and my kids. With them, there are no surprises about values. No exit disagreements. No one is pulling for a quick flip while I'm building for the next generation.

Theresa and I have been aligned for over three decades. We didn't always agree on paint colors or whether to upgrade kitchens, but we always agreed on the mission: build long-term wealth and financial freedom.

Now, my kids are part of that vision too. They're learning the discipline, the patience, and the mindset that will keep our family's wealth intact for generations.

That's partnership. Not a handshake over beers. Not a cousin swearing he'll put in sweat equity. Partnership for me is my immediate family—and immediate family only. Basically, this is going it alone because we are a unit.

TOOLKIT – AVOIDING THE PARTNERSHIP TRAP

Rule of thumb: If you hesitate on any of those answers, don't partner.

1. **Partnership Red Flags**
    - Different timelines (you want twenty years; they want two).
    - Unequal work ethic (one works; one coasts).
    - Cash vs. equity misalignment (one needs cash flow now; one wants appreciation).
    - Exit disagreements (one wants to sell; one wants to hold).
2. **Solo Success Habits**
    - Build your own Analyzer and rely on it—not a partner's opinion.
    - Pay vendors the same day; loyalty builds speed.
    - Document everything—leases, expenses, inspections.
    - Keep decision-making centralized—you.
3. **Safe Alternatives to Partnerships**
    - Hire employees or contractors instead of splitting ownership.
    - Use lenders: banks, private money, or even short-term investors—but structure it as debt, not equity.
    - Create family partnerships with aligned values and timelines.
4. **Questions to Ask Before Ever Saying Yes**

- If this person wanted to exit in twelve months, what would happen?
- Am I willing to lose this relationship if things go bad?
- Do we have exactly the same definition of success?

Going it alone doesn't mean doing everything by yourself. It means owning the accountability. You make the decisions. You shoulder the risk. And when you succeed, you don't have to argue about who deserves what.

It also means building the right support team: your roofer, plumber, electrician, banker, and attorney. People you pay fairly and quickly. People who trust you and show up. People who tell you the truth, not what you want to hear.

That's how you "go it alone" without actually being alone.

So, the lesson is simple: build alone, but protect together. Build your empire with discipline, and then safeguard it with structure so your kids and grandkids inherit not just wealth, but peace.

THE EMPLOYEE VS. INVESTOR MINDSET

This was also the moment my mindset began to shift.

Up until then, I thought like an employee: work, get paid, save. My financial life was tied directly to my job. But buying an income-producing property meant my money would now work for me. I wouldn't just trade hours for dollars. I'd trade dollars for assets that generated income on their own.

It was a leap. I worried about tenants trashing the place, about covering the mortgage, about losing it all. But I kept circling back to the same question: *What if it works?*

THE SEARCH & THE FIRST DEAL

With rules established, the search began.

Craig, my real estate agent, scheduled showing after showing. In a short span, we toured about twenty properties. The range was wide:

- Some were structural disasters
- Some had nonpaying tenants
- Some were priced for fantasy

But I wasn't discouraged. Every property was practiced. Out of twenty, six earned offers. Most were rejected immediately. That didn't bother me. Rejection is feedback, not failure.

I had another advantage I didn't fully appreciate at the time: mechanical confidence. My father taught me to use tools, solve problems, and not panic when things broke. My friend Anthony was equally capable.

That mattered. Renovation costs can make or break early deals. Sweat equity—used wisely—creates margin.

Eventually, one property stood out: a four-family building with a detached garage rented separately. Five income streams. One roof. The numbers worked—comfortably.

Monthly Income

Four-family property with detached garage rented separately. Five income streams. One roof.

Unit 1	$1,390
Unit 2	$1,200
Unit 3	$1,000
Unit 4	$800
Garage	$200
Total	**$4,590**

Monthly Expenses

Mortgage (15-year fixed)	$2,516
Taxes	$750
Insurance	$180
Maintenance Reserve *Adjust up or down based on the condition of the building.*	$200
Water / Sewer	$80
Total Expenses	**$3,726**
Net Cash Flow	**$863**

Cash flow exceeded expectations. Expenses were conservative. Tenants were paying the mortgage, and equity was building monthly. That was my first true encounter with leverage—not theoretical but lived. That was my light bulb moment: not only was the mortgage getting paid down, but I was pocketing nearly $900 per month while my tenants were building me equity.

I didn't realize it at the time, but this was the first taste of leverage, using other people's money to build my wealth.

MOMENTUM: THE UNEXPECTED SECOND DEAL

Three weeks after closing, I received a call I didn't expect.

A seller I had previously made an offer to reached out. His buyer fell through. Did I still want the property?

I said no. I had just closed my first deal and planned to wait a year.

He called again. I declined again.

By the third call, desperation was obvious. I threw out a number so low I expected the conversation to end.

He accepted.

My heart dropped.

I walked into the house that night with pizza and flowers. My wife immediately knew something was off.

That deal taught me about motivated sellers. Motivation isn't interest—it's urgency. When urgency appears, leverage shifts.

It also taught me something else: opportunity doesn't respect your timeline. It arrives when it arrives. Prepared investors capitalize. Hesitant investors rationalize.

TEACHING MOMENT: MOTIVATED SELLERS

A motivated seller isn't just someone interested in selling. It's someone who *needs* to sell... and fast. Here are some signs I now look for:

- Relocation deadlines
- Vacant properties bleeding cash
- Financial distress
- Repeated follow-ups

As for making offers, here's my rule: no offer is too insulting. Sometimes that's exactly how you land a steal of a deal. A lot of my first offers are far below asking, and here's one that really stands out.

The property was listed at $790,000. I offered $504,000. The realtor flat-out told me it was insulting. I reminded her that legally she was required to present it to the seller, and I had a strong feeling the owner needed to unload.

Sure enough, she called me back later that night. She was shocked, but the seller had countered at $590,000. I didn't flinch. I told her my absolute max was $513,000 and gave a deadline: five hours to accept, or I was moving on to another deal.

He accepted.

Here's the kicker: my Analyzer valued the property at $665,000 using my standard 1% over the current interest rate for a mortgage. That's why I always say no offer is too low or too insulting because if you stick to your numbers and stay disciplined, you can sometimes land a deal most people would think is impossible. My wife tells me to stop being so difficult, but the truth is, I love the art of the deal. There's something about the process that lights me up. I get a flood of energy that lasts for days. Negotiating, pushing the limits, finding that hidden angle, it's exhilarating. And here's the point: great deals are always out there. You just can't be afraid to get creative or to throw out a low number. As you'll see throughout this book, some of my biggest home runs started with offers others would've laughed at.

Fear is temporary. Regret is permanent

When you recognize motivation, you don't rush—you structure carefully. Motivation creates opportunity, but discipline determines outcome.

Before those deals, I assumed real estate would be slow—one property every few years. I was wrong.

Momentum builds confidence. Confidence builds decisiveness. Decisiveness attracts opportunity.

I learned a lesson that shaped everything that followed:

When the numbers work and the deal is right, you need to act. Fear is temporary. Regret is permanent.

KEY LESSONS FROM MY FIRST TWO DEALS

Those early deals taught me lessons no book could:

- Systems protect beginners - Always run the numbers before falling in love with a property.
- Cash flow creates confidence
- Multiple income streams stabilize risk
- Credit is leverage's foundation
- Lifestyle discipline accelerates progress

I wasn't just buying property. I was building a repeatable system. And once the system worked, everything changed. One of the most important lessons I learned early on was the value of credit. Your credit score is more than just a number; it's your financial reputation. A strong score opens doors, lowers interest rates, and makes banks eager to work with you. I can't stress this enough: never miss a payment, never be late, and never take your credit for granted. Treat it like gold, because in the eyes of lenders, it is.

The other key principle is lifestyle discipline. There's a time to reward yourself, but never live beyond your means or spend recklessly. Too many people sabotage their future wealth by chasing short-term pleasures. Instead, I chose to live strategically, keeping my focus on building long-term assets. Banks need to lend money—that's their business model—and when you pair strong credit with smart financial habits, they'll line up to give it to you.

Those early days were nerve-wracking, but they also set the tone for everything that came after. I wasn't just buying properties; I was building a system. And once the system worked, I never looked back.

The first deals teach courage. The next phase teaches scale.

In the next chapter, we move deeper into financing, leverage, and the decisions that determine whether you build slowly—or compress decades into years.

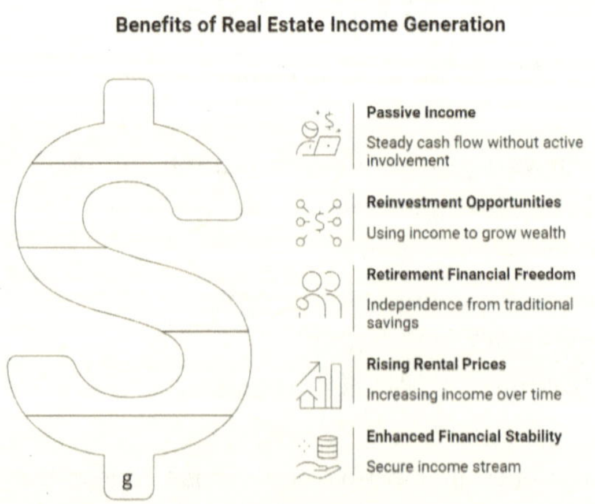

CHAPTER 3
FINANCING & GROWING YOUR PORTFOLIO

Most people never buy their first investment property for one reason: They don't have enough money.

I believed that too—until I realized how incomplete that thought really was.

When I started, I did things the "responsible" way. I saved. I waited for bonus checks. I put money down and took out fifteen-year fixed-rate mortgages. That approach worked—and for a while, it felt safe.

Safety, however, is often the most expensive choice you can make.

At first, my goal wasn't speed. It was certain. I wanted to know that every property could survive worst-case scenarios. That mindset wasn't wrong—but it was incomplete.

What I eventually learned is this: The way you finance deals determines how fast—or how slowly—you build wealth.

Financing is not just a mechanical step. It's a philosophy. By strategically refinancing and pulling equity from properties, I was able to buy more buildings while still holding on to my original assets. That's when I truly understood the value of *great debt*. And in real estate, great debt is what builds empires.

The way you finance deals determines how fast—or how slowly—you build wealth.

Early on, I relied on savings and bonuses. It worked—but it was slow. Back then, I was so focused on staying debt-free that I missed opportunities. I didn't refinance, I didn't leverage equity, and as a result, I grew slower than I could have. Eventually, I learned that capital isn't the real constraint. Creativity is. I discovered the magic of leverage. By strategically refinancing and pulling equity from properties, I was able to buy more buildings while still holding on to my original assets. That's when I truly understood there's not just good debt *and* bad debt. There's also *great debt.* And in real estate, great debt is what builds empires.

There are many ways to fund deals:

- Traditional bank loans
- FHA house hacking
- Assumable loans
- Seller financing
- Subject-to deals
- DSCR loans
- HELOCs and refinances
- Structured partnerships

1. Traditional Bank Financing

This is the most straightforward route. You put down 20–25% of the purchase price, and the bank finances the rest with a mortgage.

Pros	Cons
Stability	High upfront cash required
Best interest rates	Strict underwriting
Credibility with sellers	Longer approval process

2. FHA Loans – TAKE Advantage of This!

Federal Housing Administration (FHA) loans allow you to put down as little as 3.5%, as long as you live in one of the units for at least one year. This is the backbone of the house hack strategy.

Pros	Cons
Low down payment	Must live on-site
Easier to qualify	Requires PMI (mortgage insurance), which adds cost
	Limited to four units

I will say this: take advantage of the first-time homebuyers' program. When people ask me, "If you could go back and do one thing differently in your twenties, what would it be?" my answer is simple: I would have taken full advantage of the **first-time homebuyer programs**—before marriage, before kids, before life got complicated.

Most people miss this opportunity because they don't even know it exists, or they assume they can't afford to buy without a huge savings account. That's a myth. With an **FHA loan**, you only need **3.5% down** on a one- to four-family home. That means if you're buying a $400,000 property, you only need $14,000 to get started. Not nothing—but a lot less than the $80,000 you'd need for a traditional 20% down payment.

Here's where the real power comes in: if you're single or engaged, each of you can take advantage of this program separately. Once you're married, you've used up the "first-time" card. But if you do it before, both of you can buy your own 1–4 family property. Then, after marriage, you're sitting on **two properties** instead of one—and you got into both with minimal down payments.

Why one to four families?

Because FHA allows it. A single-family is fine, but the magic is in **multifamily properties**:

You live in one unit.

You rent out the others.

The rent covers most (or all) of your mortgage.

This is called **house hacking**, and it's one of the smartest ways to jump-start wealth.

Let's run a quick example:

You buy a **four-family property** for $500,000 with 3.5% down.

That's only **$17,500 down** (plus closing costs).

Your mortgage, taxes, and insurance are around $3,200/month.

You live in one unit. The other three rent for $1,200 each = **$3,600/month**.

Boom—your tenants are paying the mortgage while you build equity.

Now imagine your fiancé or partner does the same thing. That's **two four-family homes**—eight total units—and you're living for nearly free while the tenants are building your wealth.

BUYING A HOUSE: THE MOST CONTROVERSIAL TOPIC IN PERSONAL FINANCE

Buying a house is one of the most emotional—and controversial—topics in personal finance. Everyone has an opinion. Parents push it. Banks encourage it. Realtors celebrate it. Society treats it like a rite of passage.

So let me say this clearly upfront:

If your goal is to become wealthy—and free from economic anxiety—buying a house early is usually the wrong move.

A primary residence is not an asset in the wealth-building stage of your life. It does not put money in your pocket. It does the opposite—it dramatically increases your monthly expenses and pulls your capital out of the market at the exact time your money should be working the hardest for you.

When you buy a house, you don't just buy the house.

You remove tens—or hundreds—of thousands of dollars from your financial army. Money that could have been buying income-producing assets. Money that could have been compounding. Money that could have been growing while you sleep.

Once that cash goes into a house, it's locked. It's no longer working for you.

And the costs don't stop at the mortgage.

Now you've added property taxes. Insurance. Water. Sewer. Utilities. Possibly HOA dues. Then comes furnishing the house—another pile of debt disguised as "necessities."

And it never ends.

That outdated teal bathtub has to go. The walls need paint. The kitchen looks tired. Suddenly renovations become "mandatory." Then you need tools. Lawn equipment. Garbage cans. Snow shovels. A mower. A blower. A never-ending list of things draining cash every month.

I see this all the time.

We have close family friends whose kids recently got married. Like most parents from older generations, the advice was immediate:

"Go buy a house—here's some money for the down payment."

That advice worked decades ago.

Those days are gone.

Back then, the formula was simple: get a job, buy a mini-van, buy a house, and life worked out. Today, that same formula often leads straight into financial stress.

Here's what usually happens:

They go to the bank.

They go to a realtor.

Both ask the same two questions:

"How much do you make?" and "How much do you have saved?"

Then they show you the *maximum house you can afford*, not the smartest house to buy.

Everyone's excited. They feel accomplished.

But no one talks about the renovations.

No one talks about maintenance.

No one talks about emergencies.

And emergencies always show up right when you think you're finally getting ahead.

A roof fails—there's $20,000.

A septic system goes—there's $25,000.

A water heater blows.

A furnace dies.

The list never ends.

Now you're locked into debt, stressed, living paycheck to paycheck—and your dream of financial independence quietly disappears.

This is the downward cycle society pushes you into.

Mortgage.

Bills.

Repairs.

More debt.

More stress.

My advice?

Buy your dream house later.

Buy your "forever home" when you already have assets working for you.

Buy it when you have real financial margin—when you have what I call *"I don't need this paycheck" money.*

Until then, fight the urge to fit in.

Instead, I urge you to do something far smarter:

House hack.

Buy a 2–4 family property.

Live in one unit.

Let the other tenants help pay the mortgage.

Build equity.

Learn the business.

Then repeat.

That strategy allows you to own real estate without suffocating your cash flow. It turns your housing expense into a wealth-building vehicle instead of a financial anchor.

Yes, people will argue that housing prices have risen 200–300% since the 80s and 90s—and they're right.

But timing matters.

Your early years are not for comfort.

They are for compounding.

Those are the years when your money should be multiplying, not sitting trapped inside drywall and granite countertops.

Build assets first.

Buy the house later.

That's how you eliminate economic anxiety—and buy freedom instead.

If you start your marriage by house hacking two one- to four-family homes, you're not starting with expenses; you're starting with assets.

And here's the best part: once you move into one property together, you can rent out your other unit. Suddenly, you've created multiple income streams before your first anniversary. That's not just smart; that's transformational.

WHAT HAPPENS AFTER THE FIRST ONE

Here's the catch: after you use your FHA first-time program, you can't do it again. From that point on, most lenders will require a **20% down payment** for investment properties. That's why this window—before you're married—is golden.

After the first two, the game changes. You'll need to save more, refinance, or leverage equity. But if you and your spouse start with **two FHA loans on four-family homes**, you already have the foundation to snowball into bigger deals.

3. Assumable Loans

An assumable loan lets you take over the seller's existing mortgage at the same rate and terms. In today's market, where some loans still carry ultra-low interest rates, this can be a game-changer.

Pros	Cons
Lock in financing terms that may no longer exist	May still need cash to cover the seller's equity, but may be able to do some seller financing to cover the equity

4. Seller Financing

Instead of going to a bank, with seller financing, you make payments directly to the seller. They become the lender. The terms (down payment, rate, amortization) are all negotiable. For example, if the seller wants $500,000, you might negotiate $50,000 down and the rest paid over ten years at 6%.

Pros	Cons
Flexibility	Not every seller is open to it
Bypass banks	Requires strong contracts and legal documentation
Steady income for the seller	

5. "Subject To" Financing

You buy the property subject to the existing mortgage. The title transfers to you, but the loan stays in the seller's name. You take over payments without creating a new loan.

Pros	Cons
Lock in financing terms that may no longer exist	May still need cash to cover the seller's equity, but may be able to do some seller financing to cover the equity

"Financing is not just a mechanical step — it's a philosophy. By strategically refinancing and pulling equity from properties, I was able to buy more buildings while still holding on to my original assets. That's when I truly understood the value of great debt. And in real estate, great debt is what builds empires."

6. DSCR Loans (Debt Service Coverage Ratio)

These loans are based on the property's income, not your personal income. As long as rent covers the mortgage and expenses with a cushion, you can qualify.

Pros	Cons
Great for investors with multiple properties	Higher interest rates than conventional loans
Less focus on personal debt-to-income	Stricter coverage ratios

7. Hard Money Loans

Short-term, asset-based loans are used for flips or heavy rehabs. They're expensive but fast and flexible.

Pros	Cons
Quick approval	Very high interest rates
Flexible for distressed properties	Short payback window

8. Partnerships & Joint Ventures (with caution)

If you don't have the down payment, you can bring in a partner. You provide the deal, sweat equity, or management skills, and they provide the capital. Together, you split profits.

Pros	Cons
Scale faster with less cash	Shared control
Access to partner's capital, expertise, or workload	Potential partnership disputes
	Long-term equity dilution

SAVING VS. INVESTING: BUILDING ASSETS

Saving feels responsible. Investing feels risky. That's the illusion. Saving preserves money. Investing multiplies it.

When I was growing up, the mantra Save your money was everywhere. Teachers said it. Parents repeated it. Society reinforced it. The formula was simple: work hard, stash away part of your paycheck, and one day—if you were lucky—you could retire.

The problem? There are two reasons why saving alone will never set you free. One, bank interest rates are minimal. Savings accounts pay pennies compared to inflation. Earning 2–3% in a savings account while inflation eats 3–4% per year means you're quietly losing money. Two, inflation is stealing your money. It punishes idle capital quietly. Every year, your money buys less—even if the balance grows. It's the rise in prices over time, so a dollar saved today buys less tomorrow. If inflation averages 3%, your $100,000 loses a third of its purchasing power in fifteen years. Saving you money in a money market or savings account gives you the illusion of safety because it's insured by the federal government, but the reality is that "safety" locks you into slow decline.

Investing, on the other hand, multiplies your money. It creates leverage. It puts every dollar to work. And no vehicle has done that better for me than real estate.

I still remember holding my first little blue bank book. My parents encouraged me to deposit my birthday money, lawn-cutting money, and holiday money. At the end of the year, the balance showed a few dollars of interest—$1.37.

At ten years old, that seemed like magic. Free money! But by the time I was an adult, I realized the cruel truth: saving alone wasn't building wealth. It was treading water at best, sinking at worst.

My father lived the disciplined life his generation was taught to admire. He went to college, landed a steady job, and worked hard for decades. Every two weeks, his paycheck showed up without fail. He saved diligently, contributed to his retirement plan, and lived within his means. In many ways, he lived the American Dream as society defined it—predictable, respectable, safe. I respect that deeply, and I'm grateful for the example of discipline and responsibility he gave me.

But here's what I saw as I got older: that version of success came with chains, not wings. My father exchanged his time for money year after year. Vacations were rare, stress was constant, and the idea of retirement was always dangled far in the future. When he finally reached it, the best years of his health and freedom were already behind him.

He was proud of me when I followed in his footsteps, earning degrees, climbing the corporate ladder, and getting promotions. But while I was proud of him for the sacrifices he made, I knew I wanted more than stability. I wanted freedom. I wanted freedom from someone dictating my schedule, capping my income, or pulling the rug out from under me with one HR meeting. That conflict between the security I was taught and the freedom I craved wasn't easy to face. But it forced me to confront the truth: a paycheck alone was not security.

I watched capable professionals lose jobs overnight. Stability vanished instantly.

Fresh out of USC with a master's in health administration, I thought I had landed the dream job. I was working at one of the most prestigious academic medical centers in the world. The title was impressive, the pay was solid, and the career path looked promising. I worked long hours, poured myself into building a new business platform, and we were succeeding.

Too much, in fact. The program grew faster than expected, generating revenue and empowering physicians. But in large institutions, success can threaten people who feel their power slipping. Politics crept in. Decisions became less about logic and more about egos.

I'll never forget walking into that mahogany-paneled boardroom. Twenty people sat around the table, tension thick in the air. After a heavy silence, one of the deans said the words that still echo in my memory: "We are shutting the company down." Just like that, it was over. Millions of dollars and countless hours of work vanished. Severance checks were handed out, and my "safe" job disappeared overnight.

That was the day the illusion of job security shattered for me. A paycheck felt safe only until someone else decided it wasn't. Real security doesn't come from a title or a company. It comes from assets, things that generate income whether you're in the office or not. Assets don't fire you. Assets don't hold closed-door meetings to decide your fate. Assets don't care about politics. They just keep producing.

That wake-up call lit a fire in me. From that day on, I was determined never again to let my family's future depend on someone else's decision in a boardroom.

Assets don't eliminate risk—but they shift control back to you.

This became my personal rule. Assets—real estate, businesses, and later, index funds, and life insurance policies that produce cash flow and appreciate—came first. Liabilities—cars, watches, vacations, and boats—would have to wait. They're nice, but only once the assets are in place to fund them.

It's easy to get this backward. Most people chase the appearance of success—fancy cars, designer clothes, expensive vacations—while their balance sheet is drowning in debt. I saw it all the time in corporate America: colleagues with six-figure salaries who looked wealthy on the outside but were broke on the inside. The second their job disappeared, so did their lifestyle.

Assets come first. Liabilities have to wait

When you build assets first, the story flips. Assets create income. Income buys freedom. And freedom, when the time is right, buys the liabilities without stress, debt, or fear. That's real wealth.

The average cost of a multifamily home in the US is $500,000. Older stock in less expensive cities might go for $300,000 to $500,000 while in big metros or high-rent areas it could easily be $700,000 to $1 million plus, but rents are commensurate with price. Let's run through a conservative scenario to illustrate the difference between saving and investing.

Suppose you buy a multi-family property worth $500,000. You put down $100,000 and finance the rest. Over fifteen years, let's assume the property appreciates at a conservative rate of 8% annually.

Future Value (FV) Calculation:

$$\mathbf{Fv=500{,}000 \times (1+ 0.08)15:}$$
$$\mathbf{Fv = 500{,}000 \times 3.172}$$
$$\mathbf{FCV \approx 1{,}586{,}00}$$

In fifteen years, your $500,000 property is now worth $1.586 million.

Your initial $100,000 down payment has turned into over $1.086 million in equity—and that doesn't even count the rental income you've been collecting or the fact that tenants helped pay down your mortgage.

Now let's look at what would have happened if you simply saved that same $100,000 in a traditional vehicle.

Vehicle	15-Year Value	Growth from $100k
Savings (2%)	$134,000	+$34,000
Bonds (4%)	$180,000	+$80,000
Index Fund (8%)	$317,000	+$217,000
Real Estate (leveraged)	$1,086,000+	+$986,000+

Sounds decent, right? But compare that to $1,086,000 in equity—a 10x difference—and they aren't really in the same ballpark. That's the power of leverage in real estate. With investing, your money grows in multiple ways:

1. **Appreciation** (property value increases).
2. **Cash Flow** (rental income every month).
3. **Loan Paydown** (your tenants pay off your mortgage).
4. **Tax Advantages** (deductions, depreciation, capital gains strategies—more on this in the chapter 5).

(A simple line graph showing the curve of savings, bonds, stocks, and real estate. Real estate skyrockets while the others crawl upward.)

Saving is important for emergencies and short-term goals. You need an emergency fund (three to six months of expenses). But it will never create financial freedom. You're saving for a short-term purchase (car, wedding, down payment within one to three years). Investing—especially in real estate—creates leverage, cash flow, and generational wealth. Investing is essential when:

- You're building long-term wealth.
- You want passive income.
- You want to hedge against inflation.
- You're planning for retirement or generational wealth.

Your money should be working harder than you do. That's how you escape the cycle of working until sixty-seven and finally "retiring." Investing, not saving, is the road to freedom.

Here's a real-world example of how powerful real estate can be when you combine cash flow, appreciation, and time. In 2015, I purchased a three-family investment property for **$250,000**. I put **$50,000 down** and financed the rest. From day one, the property cash-flowed approximately **$1,800 per month**, or **$21,600 per year**. Fast forward to today, and that same property was recently appraised for **$765,000**.

Let's break down the return.

On the **cash-on-cash side**, I invested $50,000 and earned $21,600 per year. That's a **43.2% annual cash-on-cash return** ($21,600 ÷ $50,000), before even factoring in rent increases over time.

Now let's look at **equity growth**. The property increased in value by **$515,000** ($765,000–$250,000). Even before accounting for loan paydown, that appreciation alone represents a **1,030% return** on my original $50,000 investment.

And here's the part most people miss: **tenants paid the mortgage the entire time**. I didn't have to save extra money to create that equity—it happened automatically while the property produced income every month.

This is why real estate works. One investment produced **monthly cash flow, massive appreciation, forced savings through loan amortization**, and **leverage-driven returns** that simply don't exist in traditional savings or retirement accounts. This is how ordinary people build extraordinary wealth—one disciplined deal at a time.

SCALING VS. HOLDING: THE FASTEST PATH TO WEALTH

If there's one principle that separates average landlords from true wealth-builders, it's this: understanding leverage. This chapter isn't about owning a couple of rentals so you can supplement retirement. It's about multiplying. It's about seeing the hidden potential in every dollar—then sending that dollar back into the field again and again. Most people never take this step. They stay in the "buy one, pay it off, feel safe" mindset. But real wealth in real estate comes from leverage, scale, and the patience to play the long game.

When I first started out, I was convinced I had the formula. Buy one multi-family, put it on a fifteen-year mortgage, pay it off, and live on the income. Safe. Predictable. Responsible. And for a while, that plan made sense. My wife and I were learning as we went, and safety felt like wisdom. But I was wrong.

Holding a single property for fifteen years will build some wealth. You'll likely end up with a valuable asset and solid cash flow. But compared to what's possible when you put equity to work—when you refinance smartly and scale—it's a fraction of the potential. My early mindset was limiting. I thought safety meant freedom, when in reality it kept me stuck.

Here's a hard truth I had to accept: Being debt-free too early slowed my growth. I didn't refinance when I should have. I didn't leverage appreciation. I played defense when offense was appropriate. Once I understood leverage properly, everything changed. Fixed-rate debt plus rising rents equals inflation working for you.

Being debt-free too early can slow your growth.

Scaling isn't reckless—it's structured.

Picture two investors starting at the same point. Both buy their first rental in Year 0. Investor A—the Debt-Free Devotee—hates debt. Every spare dollar goes toward paying off the mortgage. After fifteen years, they own one property free and clear. It's stable, it's comfortable, and it works—just slowly. Investor B—the Multiplier—sees equity as an opportunity. After five years, they refinance, pull out cash, and buy more. Five years later, they do it again. By Year 15, instead of one roof, they own many. The same time horizon, the same starting line, but very different destinations.

THE PSYCHOLOGICAL SHIFT THAT UNLOCKS GROWTH

This chapter isn't really about financing. It's about identity. You stop asking: "Is this safe?" And start asking: "Is this managed?" You stop hoarding certainty and start building systems. Banks don't hate debt.

They hate chaos. When your numbers are clean, your structure is sound, and your discipline is proven, capital becomes available.

No mortgage looks safe on paper. But equity sitting in a property is lazy money. It earns nothing beyond modest appreciation. Inflation eats into its buying power. Opportunity cost compounds. By avoiding all risk, some investors end up taking the biggest risk of all: missing compounding growth.

Try to borrow 80% to buy stocks. The bank will show you the door. Try the same with a rental property. Now they're interested. Real estate is tangible, cash-flowing, and collateralized. That's why banks lend against it, and that's why leverage works here when it doesn't in most other asset classes.

WHY INACTION COSTS MORE THAN MISTAKES

Here's the truth: mistakes are expensive, but inaction is devastating. You can recover from a bad deal—you learn, you adjust, you move forward. But you can't recover the years you wasted waiting for the "perfect" moment.

While you hesitate, property values climb. While you hesitate, rents rise. While you hesitate, equity compounds—for someone else.

That's why I always say: **imperfect action beats perfect inaction.**

Stuck in Corporate Life

I have other friends who are brilliant, hard-working people. They grind day in and day out, loyal employees to massive corporations. And every two weeks, the paycheck arrives—minus 35%. That's right: at least four months of the year, they're working for free, just to pay Uncle Sam.

That's the system. School, society, and employers train you to be a cog in their wheel. Work hard. Collect a check. Pay your taxes. Retire at sixty-seven. And maybe, if you're lucky, you'll get to enjoy what's left of your life.

But here's the thing: that's not freedom. That's survival. And I didn't want survival. I wanted a **choice.**

So I built assets. I used tax strategies. I made my money work harder than I ever could. Yes, my employer helped along the way—but I knew I had to get off that train.

If you're stuck in corporate life, here's my advice: use it while you can, but plan your exit. Don't give your best years to someone else's dream.

THE WEALTH FORMULA

Cash Flow + Appreciation + Tax Benefits + Leverage = Real Estate Wealth

Cash flow keeps you liquid and resilient. Appreciation turns time into equity. Tax benefits keep more money in your pocket. Leverage is the multiplier that turns one property into many. Think in all four dimensions—not just one.

1. Buy property that cash flows from Day 1.
2. Hold it for three to five years while tenants pay down the loan and the market appreciates.
3. Refinance—pull out equity tax-free (the government does not tax debt)—and keep the property.
4. Use the cash to buy another property.
5. Repeat every five years. Do this patiently, and the snowball becomes an avalanche.

With fixed-rate debt, your payment stays the same while rents and values rise. Inflation quietly shrinks the real cost of your mortgage every year, even as your income grows. Used wisely, debt isn't a burden—it's a tool.

By the time many people save enough to buy a property outright, the market has moved. Prices are higher, rents are higher, and they've missed years of appreciation and amortization. The investor who used leverage already owns multiple appreciating assets.

FINAL THOUGHT: STOP READING, START DOING

This book was written as a **roadmap**—not as entertainment. If you just read it, you'll finish with nothing but highlighted pages. If you act on it, you'll finish with a different life.

Sacrifice now, so your family reaps later. Work for yourself, not the system. And above all—**don't waste twenty years making excuses.**

Because if I could really borrow that time machine from *Back to the Future,* I wouldn't go back to relive my wins. I'd go back to tell myself one thing: *Take action. Now.*

I've been at this game for over twenty-five years, and I can't tell you how many friends of mine are still stuck saying the same thing: *"Glenn, I'm getting closer."* But year after year, it's the same excuses—like the grown-up version of *"my dog ate my homework."*

In the next chapter, we'll look at the power of using other people's money responsibly.

CHAPTER 4
THE POWER OF LEVERAGE

When I first started out, I didn't truly understand the power of leverage. In fact, I avoided it. Like most people, I had been raised with the belief that debt is bad—that owing money meant risk, stress, and danger. So I saved, paid cash when I could, and took pride in staying debt-free. I fell into the same trap most of Main Street does: listening to everyone around me instead of thinking for myself.

What I didn't realize then was that there's a huge difference between bad debt and good debt.

- **Bad debt** buys things that lose value the minute you swipe your card — cars, furniture, vacations, gadgets.
- **Good debt**, on the other hand, buys assets that generate income and appreciate over time, such as real estate.

When you understand how to use debt strategically, it becomes leverage. And leverage is how ordinary people build extraordinary wealth.

LEARNING THE HARD WAY

The term *leverage* gets tossed around a lot, but here's the truth: leverage multiplies whatever you already are. If you're disciplined, patient, and calculated, leverage accelerates your wealth. If you're reckless, emotional, and impatient, leverage accelerates your losses.

Early in my career, I didn't use leverage as aggressively as I could have, and that slowed my growth. But I also saw what being over-leveraged can do, and it's not pretty.

THE VERONA STORY – A LESSON IN OVERLEVERAGE

A perfect example came from a deal I chased in Verona, New Jersey. There was an investor named Silvio who had bought three apartment buildings over five years, all at the height of the market. He was aggressive, buying with short-term, high-leverage loans—mostly three-year balloon mortgages—and almost no reserves.

On paper, it looked impressive. In reality, he was walking a financial tightrope. His rents barely covered the expenses, and the buildings weren't appreciating fast enough to bail him out. When the balloon mortgage came due, his rates went up two full percentage points. That pushed his payments higher, his cash flow negative, and his stress through the roof.

He called me one day in a panic, wanting to unload one of the buildings—the Verona property. I ran my numbers and made him an offer, roughly $350,000 less than what he had paid. He was offended. "Glenn, I can't take that kind of loss," he said.

"You're already taking it. You just haven't admitted it yet."

He had no reserves, no margin, and no flexibility. He was fully leveraged to the hilt and trapped by his own deals. I walked away. A few months later, I found out his parents bailed him out and paid down the loans so he could breathe again. Good for him, but not everyone has parents who can write a six-figure check to save the day.

That deal taught me a permanent lesson: leverage is a tool, not a lifeline. Use it strategically, not emotionally.

THE GOLDEN RULES OF LEVERAGE

Over the years, I built my own playbook for responsible leverage — principles I still follow today:

1. **Only Buy Cash-Flowing Properties.**
2. If the property doesn't pay you every month, don't buy it. Future appreciation is a bonus, not a bailout.

3. **Keep Reserves.**
4. Always have a cushion — at least six months of mortgage payments and operating expenses in a separate account. Murphy's Law loves real estate.
5. **Avoid Over-Leveraging.**
6. Stay in the 65–75% Loan-to-Value (LTV) range. That's the sweet spot between growth and stability.
7. **Diversify.**
8. Don't put all your units in one town or all your eggs in one building. Spread your risk across properties and neighborhoods.
9. **Use Fixed-Rate Debt.**
10. Variable rates can kill you. When rents rise, but your mortgage stays flat, your cash flow and cap rate improve every year.

MANAGING RISK

Leverage has risks. Rates change, tenants leave, roofs leak. Smart investors mitigate their risks. To ensure you aren't exposed to too much risk, there are a few things to keep in mind: Only buy cash-flow properties, always have some reserves, avoid overleveraging yourself, stay diversified, and try to use only fixed-rate debt.

Be sure you buy cash-flow properties. These are properties that are already rented or have a good track record of staying fully occupied. Think cash flow first and appreciation second. Be sure to

- keep reserves,
- avoid over-leveraging (stay in the 65–75% LTV lane),
- diversify across units and neighborhoods, and
- prefer fixed-rate debt.

Risk isn't something to avoid; it's something to price and manage.

Owning one or two rentals is a start. Building a portfolio is a mindset. Empire building requires vision, systems, and the humility to learn new skills—financing, management, and tax strategy. That shift from small to scalable is the real unlock.

Let's put some math behind this. Say you have $300,000 in cash. You could: buy one $300,000 property in cash or buy three $300,000 properties with 25% down each ($75,000 per property). Assume each property appreciates by 4% per year. After one year: the all-cash property gains $12,000 in value. The three leveraged properties gain $36,000 combined, even though you used the same $300,000 cash. That's leverage working in your favor. But remember, you also take on three mortgages, three roofs, and three sets of tenants. It's not free money; it's a responsibility that must be managed.

GOOD LEVERAGE VS. BAD LEVERAGE

Good Leverage	Bad Leverage
Used for cash-flowing assets	Used for consumer goods
Fixed-rate loans	Adjustable-rate or balloon loans
65–75% Loan-to-Value (LTV)	85–100% LTV
Predictable expenses, solid reserves	No reserves, high debt load
Adds to net worth	Adds to stress

WHY FIXED-RATE DEBT WINS

I can't stress this enough: fixed-rate, long-term debt is one of your biggest wealth-building allies. When inflation rises and rents climb, your mortgage payment stays the same. Every dollar of rent increase becomes pure profit, and your cash-on-cash return improves without any additional investment. Over time, leverage and inflation become your silent partners, working for you instead of against you.

The Dave Ramsey Contrast

I'll be honest—I used to listen to a lot of Dave Ramsey. He and I are on completely opposite sides of the financial spectrum. His message of living debt-free and cutting up your credit cards has helped millions of people get control of their finances, and there's real value in that. But that mindset stunted my growth early on. I avoided leverage because I thought all debt was bad. What I eventually learned is that there's a world of difference between consumer debt and strategic leverage. If I had stayed in the "no debt ever" camp, I'd still be trading time for money instead of building generational wealth.

So while Dave's plan may help you sleep at night, it won't make you truly wealthy. Playing it safe might keep you out of trouble—but it also keeps you out of opportunity. Responsible leverage, backed by strong numbers and discipline, is how you move from surviving to thriving.

THE BALANCED MINDSET

Leverage isn't something to fear, but it's not something to worship either. It's a tool and like any tool, it can build or destroy depending on how it's used.

Use my analyzer. Stick to the math. Keep reserves. And remember, banks lend to people who don't need it and foreclose on those who think they're invincible.

Smart leverage creates freedom. Over-leverage creates stress. And when you learn the difference, you stop playing defense and start playing offense in your wealth-building game.

SAFE VS. OVER-LEVERAGED REAL ESTATE OUTCOMES (10-YEAR PROJECTION)

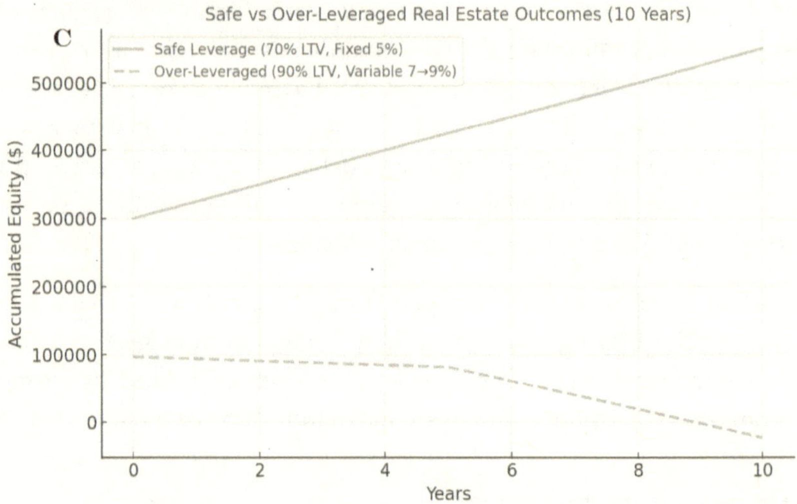

This chart shows how two investors perform over ten years. One uses safe leverage (70% LTV, fixed 5%), and one uses high leverage (90% LTV, variable 7→9%).

- The solid line shows stable, consistent equity growth — slower but safer.
- The dotted line shows what happens when over-leverage and rising rates erode cash flow and equity.

As the years pass, the investor who used disciplined, fixed-rate leverage steadily builds wealth. The over-leveraged investor, however, struggles with negative cash flow and equity stagnation once rates rise.

Lesson: Leverage can accelerate wealth, but only when used strategically. Fixed-rate, cash-flow-positive deals win the long game every time.

GENERATIONAL WEALTH: THE TRUE ENDGAME

My first small multi-family felt like a triumph. We closed, the rent checks started, and five years later, the equity looked great. But it just sat there. Then I watched peers who started around the same time refinance, pull out cash, and buy two, three, or even five more doors. I swallowed my fear, refinanced, and pulled out roughly $150,000—tax-free. It felt risky. It also changed everything.

Within months, I bought two more properties. Overnight, one roof became three. Income tripled. Five years after that, I repeated the cycle. Had I stuck with the "pay it off" plan, I'd own one property today. Instead, that decision set a chain reaction in motion. That's the multiplier effect of smart leverage.

Handing down one paid-off property is generous. Handing down a system—a diversified, cash-flowing portfolio with smart debt and tax strategy—is transformational. That's legacy.

Generational wealth is about the handoff of knowledge, structure, and mindset.

Too many people think about inheritance only in terms of a single asset: a house, a retirement account, maybe a savings plan. While those gifts matter, they don't create true freedom for the next generation. A paid-off home might save your children from ever paying rent, but it doesn't automatically teach them how to generate income, how to protect what they own, or how to expand on it.

Generational wealth is about more than a handoff of property. It's about a handoff of knowledge, structure, and mindset. If you pass down a system—one that combines real estate, cash-flowing businesses, tax strategy, and asset protection—you're not just giving your children security. You're giving them the ability to multiply what you started.

Generational wealth isn't just about passing down money—it's about passing down *readiness*. My goal was never for my kids to inherit assets and figure things out later. I want them to be able to step in without a blip, fully understanding how everything works and why it's structured the way it is. For years, and in many families even today, talking to your kids about money is treated as taboo—something secretive or off-limits. I've never believed in that. I believe in transparency. We talk openly about our finances, about what I'm doing with money and, just as importantly, what *they* are doing with theirs. I teach them how to think, how to evaluate decisions, how to manage risk, and how to build—not just spend. The truth is, money itself isn't the legacy. Knowledge is. Skills are. Systems are. If I lost everything tomorrow, I'm confident I could rebuild it—not because of luck, but because I understand the process. That's what I'm passing down to my kids. Not just assets, but the ability to create assets. That's real generational wealth.

REFINANCING: THE WEALTH MULTIPLIER

Refinancing is one of the most powerful tools in a real estate investor's playbook—if you know how and when to use it. I've refinanced dozens of properties over my career, and each time it's either saved me money, built equity faster, or unlocked capital for my next deal. The key is to treat refinancing not as a once-in-a-lifetime event, but as an active strategy for optimizing your portfolio.

1. Lower Rate or Shorter Term

One of the simplest and most effective uses of refinancing is to lower your interest rate or shorten the term of your loan. My personal rule of thumb: If I can drop my rate by at least one full percentage point, I'm running the numbers. Let's say I had a 7% mortgage and could refinance down to 6% or less. I'd move ahead because that drop can either lower my payment or, better yet, let me shorten the loan term while keeping payments nearly the same.

On one property I owned, I had a thirty-year fixed loan at 7.5%, and I refinanced it down to 5.5%. That's a two-point reduction—and I used the opportunity to move from a thirty-year to a twenty-year loan. My monthly payment stayed roughly the same, but I shaved ten years off the loan and saved over $300,000 in interest over the life of the loan.

Winner, winner, chicken dinner!

That's the kind of move that builds wealth quietly, month after month, without adding risk.

2. Cash-Out Refinancing: The Power of Equity

My favorite strategy—cash-out refinancing—is where the real magic of leverage happens. When your property appreciates, or you've paid down the loan balance, you can refinance at the higher value and pull cash out tax-free. You're not selling the property, so you don't owe capital gains. You're simply borrowing against your equity, using that capital to buy more assets.

I've done this countless times—refinance one property, take the equity, and use it as the down payment for the next deal. That's how I've scaled my portfolio over the years. It's the snowball effect of real estate: your existing assets help you acquire more, and those new assets generate income that helps pay down all your loans faster.

This is what I mean when I talk about good debt. Your tenants and your properties are doing the heavy lifting.

3. The Patience and Process

Refinancing does take time. Banks will want new appraisals, updated rent rolls, and plenty of paperwork. Be ready to explain your numbers clearly—especially if you're using DSCR (Debt Service Coverage Ratio) loans. I've had refinances take anywhere from 45 to 120 days, depending on the complexity of the deal.

But the effort is worth it. Each successful refinance either increases your cash flow, shortens your timeline to financial freedom, or funds your next acquisition—all while keeping your tax burden low.

4. Refinance Rules of Thumb

Here are a few quick guidelines I live by:

- Chase at least 1% in rate savings.
- Consider shortening the term if you can keep payments close to the same.
- Always factor in closing costs and how long it'll take to break even.
- Use cash-out refinances strategically—only to buy more income-producing assets.
- Never refinance into variable debt just to squeeze a better short-term payment.

5. The Refinance Mindset

Think of refinancing like tuning up your financial engine. You're not just chasing lower payments—you're re-optimizing your wealth machine. Whether you're locking in a lower rate, pulling equity to expand, or restructuring for better terms, each move should bring you closer to long-term financial freedom.

Refinancing isn't about chasing every shiny opportunity; it's about knowing your numbers, protecting your cash flow, and using the bank's money to multiply your own.

Refinance in Action: How a Lower Rate Builds Wealth Faster

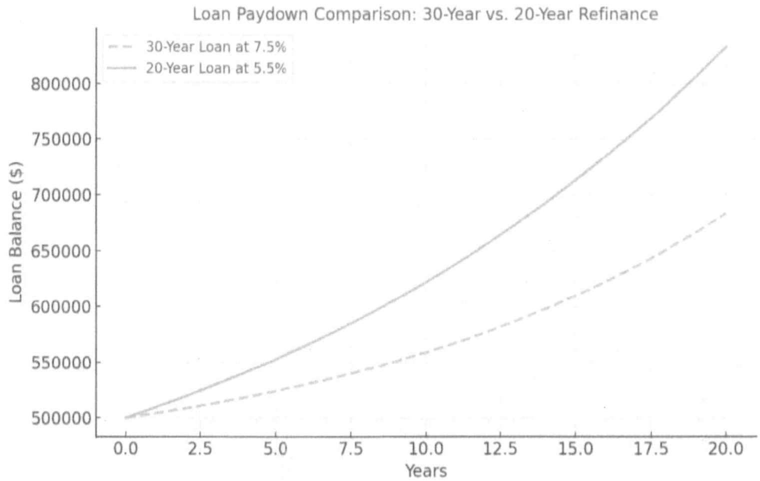

This chart compares two scenarios for a $500,000 loan:

- Scenario 1: 30-year fixed loan at 7.5%
- Scenario 2: 20-year refinance at 5.5%

The solid line shows how quickly the principal balance drops after refinancing. The difference isn't just time — it's hundreds of thousands in saved interest.

Key Insights:

- The twenty-year refinance pays off ten years sooner with nearly the same monthly payment.
- Total interest savings: Over $300,000 across the life of the loan.
- Once refinanced, every year accelerates your equity growth — and your path to financial freedom.

MORE THAN MONEY: PASSING DOWN A PLAYBOOK

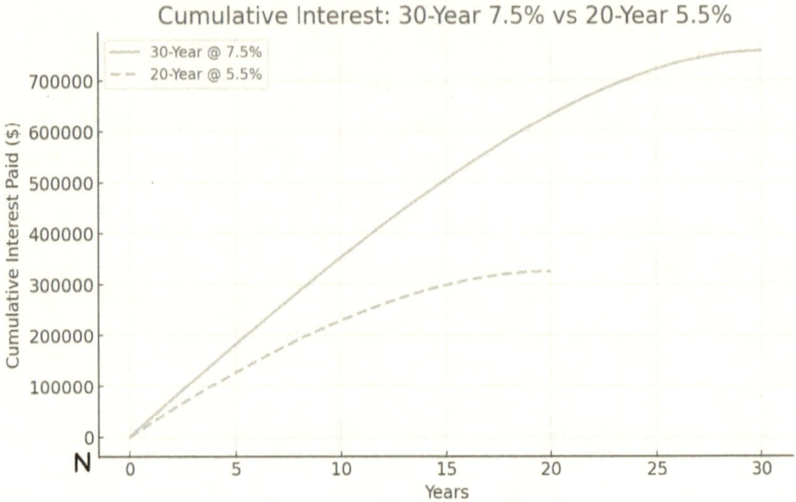

Table 1 – Portfolio Growth Snapshot

The ultra-wealthy don't simply pass down assets. They pass down a playbook. They leave behind trusts, family constitutions, and legal structures that preserve wealth for generations. They teach their children to see money not as a prize but as a tool. They establish family management companies that allow future generations to participate in the work without diluting the mission.

In my own family, I dedicate a great deal of time to this same approach. I don't just teach my kids about real estate or basic financial management. I involve them in building a framework designed to last for generations. I make it a priority to bring in subject matter experts to speak with them on topics like tax planning, portfolio strategy, wealth preservation, and asset protection. Each year, we hold a family board retreat where I schedule structured discussions around these subjects. It's a chance not only to educate but to build a shared vision for the future. In chapter 6, I dive deeper into some of the tax strategies we've discussed at those retreats and how they've helped shape our long-term plan.

Think about the difference: if your children inherit a property with no guidance, they may sell it at the first sign of difficulty. But if they inherit a system that includes

- a management company already in place,
- clear rules for reinvestment,
- tax strategies that preserve cash flow, and
- an understanding of how to expand the portfolio,

then they're positioned to not just hold onto what you built, but to grow it.

One mistake I see all the time is that people build wealth but never explain it to their kids. They keep the numbers secret or assume the next generation will just figure it out. That's a recipe for failure. If you want your children and grandchildren to continue the mission, you need to educate them as you go, like with my board retreats.

If you want your children and grandchildren to continue the mission, you need to educate them.

That doesn't mean handing them deeds when they turn eighteen. It means involving them in conversations, showing them how decisions are made, and passing along the values that guided you. Transparency is part of the legacy.

Why Systems Outlast Assets

Assets can be lost, sold, or squandered. A system is harder to destroy. With a system, your heirs inherit not just properties, but a framework for

- Evaluating deals (knowing what to buy and what to pass on).

- Managing debt wisely (understanding the difference between good leverage and destructive borrowing).
- Protecting assets (through LLCs, trusts, and insurance).
- Reinvesting cash flow (so money continues to multiply).

Ask yourself: do you want your children to simply have something of value, or do you want them to have everything they need to sustain and grow what you pass down to them? The true endgame isn't just money. It's freedom, options, and confidence for the next generation.

When you structure your wealth with systems in mind, you're not just leaving behind dollars. You're leaving behind a legacy of independence. You're ensuring that your children and grandchildren aren't just beneficiaries but builders.

That's the difference between handing down property and handing down prosperity. This is what transforms an inheritance into a dynasty.

The Roadmap Forward

Start with one. Buy for cash flow. Refinance smart. Reinvest aggressively. Repeat patiently. Build not only for yourself but for your family and the future.

Let's look at the roadmap in three tables. The first one is ...

How to Read the Roadmap

Before you dive into the numbers, I want you to understand what these tables are really showing you. This isn't theory, and it's not cherry-picked fantasy math—it's a realistic comparison of two very different mindsets applied over the same 15-year period. Both investors start in the exact same place: one property worth $500,000. Same market. Same appreciation assumptions. Same starting line. The only difference is strategy.

Investor A represents the traditional, "play it safe" approach—buy a property, hold it long term, let appreciation do the work, and avoid refinancing. There's nothing wrong with this strategy; it's stable, conservative, and familiar. Over time, the property grows in value, but the portfolio remains static.

Investor B represents the investor who understands leverage and uses it responsibly. Instead of letting equity sit idle, Investor B refinances every five years, pulls out a portion of that equity tax-free, and reinvests it into additional cash-flowing properties. The original asset is never sold—it becomes the engine that fuels the next acquisition. This process is repeated patiently and methodically, allowing the portfolio to compound rather than stagnate.

Table 1 shows the cumulative effect of these two approaches over 15 years—not just in total value, but in scale. One investor ends with a single property worth more than when they started. The other ends with nine properties and a portfolio that's nearly ten times larger. Figure 1 visually reinforces this difference, illustrating how slow, linear growth compares to exponential growth when equity is put back to work. This is the snowball effect of smart refinancing, disciplined reinvestment, and long-term thinking—and it's the foundation of how real estate becomes generational wealth, not just a retirement supplement.

Table 1

Two investors. Same starting line — one property worth $500,000 in Year 0. Investor A holds and waits. Investor B refinances every five years and redeploys the equity into more properties. Fifteen years later, the outcomes diverge dramatically.

	Investor A · Hold One Property		Investor B · Refinance & Multiply	
Year	**Properties**	**Total Value**	**Properties**	**Total Value**
0	1	$500,000	1	$500,000
5	1	$734,664	3	$2,203,992
10	1	$1,079,462	6	$6,476,775
15	**1**	**$1,586,085**	**9**	**$14,274,761**

Key reads from the scoreboard

- Same starting line. Both investors begin Year 0 with one property worth $500,000.
- Year 5. Investor B has tripled property count and is sitting on ~4× the equity. Compounding has begun.
- Year 10. Investor B owns 6 properties and ~6× Investor A's value. The gap is widening, not closing.
- Year 15. Investor B owns 9 properties worth ~$14.3M — nine times Investor A's $1.59M. Same time. Same market. Different strategy.

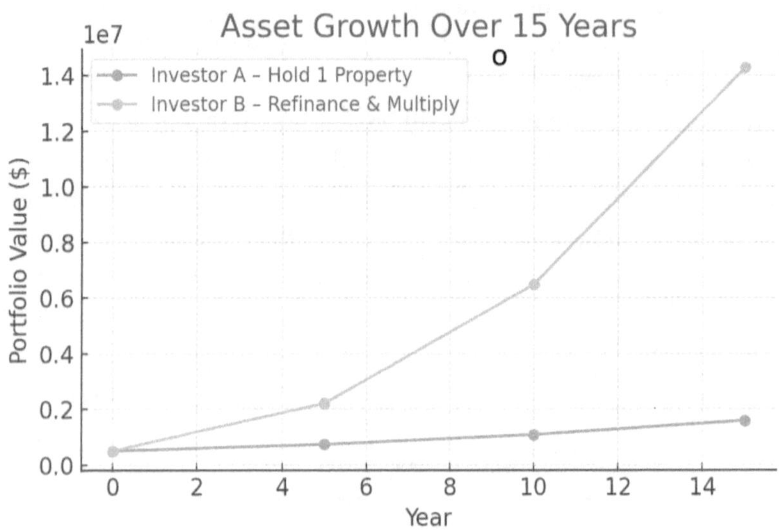

Figure 1 – Asset growth comparing a single 15-year hold vs. refinancing every five years to multiply properties.

Table 2 shows you how freedom shows up in real life—through income. This table compares the estimated gross rent generated by each investor over the same fifteen-year period. Again, both investors start in the exact same position, earning roughly $40,000 per year in gross rent from a single property. From there, the outcomes diverge sharply—not because of luck, but because of strategy.

Investor A's rent grows steadily but slowly, tracking modest appreciation and rent increases on a single property. Over time, the income improves, but it remains linear. Even after fifteen years, gross rent reaches just under $127,000 per year. That's helpful income—but it still requires careful budgeting and doesn't fully replace earned income for most households.

Investor B's income, however, compounds. Each refinance and reinvestment adds additional units, additional tenants, and additional streams of rent. As the portfolio scales, rent growth accelerates—not in a straight line, but exponentially. By year fifteen, Investor B's estimated gross rent exceeds **$1.1 million per year**, a direct result of multiplying doors rather than simply waiting for rent increases on a single asset.

Figure 2 visually reinforces this reality. What begins as a small gap becomes a widening canyon over time. This is the moment most people miss when they focus only on appreciation or net worth. Cash flow is what pays the bills, funds lifestyle, absorbs risk, and creates optionality. Scaling isn't about ego or size; it's about building income streams that are resilient, diversified, and capable of supporting not just you, but the next generation as well.

The lesson is simple but powerful: **one property can help you survive; a portfolio gives you control.**

Table 1 – Portfolio Growth Snapshot

Year	Investor A: Properties	Investor A: Total Value	Investor B: Properties	Investor B: Total Value
0	1	$500,000	1	$500,000
5	1	$734,664	3	$2,203,992
10	1	$1,079,462	6	$6,476,775
15	1	$1,586,085	9	$14,274,761

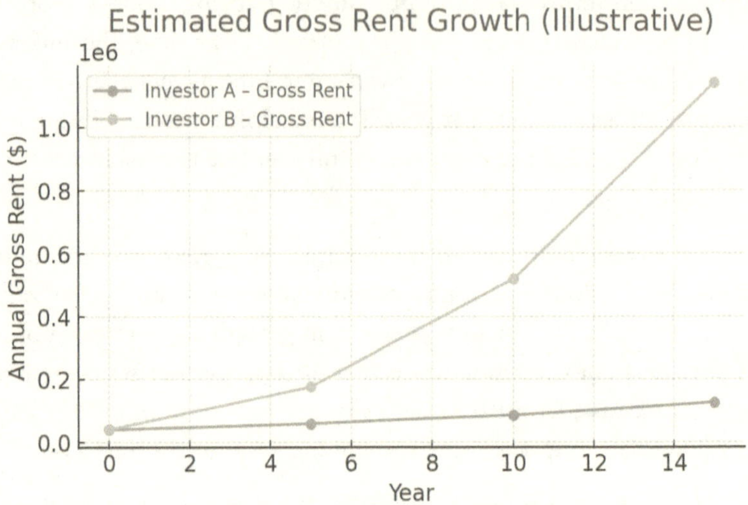

Table 2 – Estimated Gross Rent (Illustrative)

Table 3 strips everything down to what actually matters. After fifteen years, this snapshot shows the end result of two very different philosophies applied over the same time horizon. Same starting point. Same market assumptions. Radically different outcomes.

Investor A, who chose to buy and hold a single property without refinancing, ends the period owning **one property** worth roughly **$1.59 million**, producing about **$126,887 per year in gross rent**. That's not a failure—many people would be thrilled with that outcome. It represents discipline, patience, and steady progress.

But **Investor B** tells a different story. By consistently refinancing every five years and reinvesting the extracted equity, Investor B finishes year fifteen owning **nine properties**, with a combined portfolio value north of **$14.2 million** and estimated gross rents exceeding **$1.14 million per year**. That income level doesn't just supplement a lifestyle—it replaces earned income entirely and creates surplus capital for reinvestment, protection, and generational planning.

This table makes the core lesson undeniable: **time alone doesn't create wealth—strategy does**. Holding can build comfort. Scaling builds leverage, optionality, and legacy. By year fifteen, Investor B isn't just wealthier on paper; they have more control over their time, their risk, and their future dramatically. This is the difference between owning real estate and building a real estate business, and it's why the refinance-and-multiply strategy changes the game when executed with discipline.

Table 3 – Year 15 Snapshot (Bottom Line)

Metric	Investor A (Hold)	Investor B (Refi & Multiply)
Properties Owned	$1	$9
Portfolio Value	$1,586,085	$14,274,761
Est. Gross Rent/yr (~8%)	$126,887	$1,141,981

THE POWER (AND RESPONSIBILITY) OF LEVERAGE: LEVERAGE IS A MULTIPLIER, NOT A SHORTCUT.

It amplifies discipline and precision—but it can also amplify mistakes. Use it strategically, not emotionally.

1. **Good debt builds wealth; bad debt builds regret.**

Borrow for cash-flowing, income-producing assets only—never for consumption or speculation.

2. **Stay within the safety zone.**

Operate in the 65–75% Loan-to-Value range, keep six months of reserves, and lock in fixed-rate debt so your cash flow improves as rents rise.

3. **Refinance intentionally.**

Lower rates or shorter terms create silent equity. Cash-out refinancing unlocks tax-free capital to scale your portfolio — but only when the numbers justify it.

4. **Leverage is a partnership with the bank.**

Treat your lender as a business partner — because they are one. Understand their metrics, their risk tolerance, and structure deals so everyone wins.

5. **Fixed-rate debt wins the long game.**

Inflation shrinks your loan in real terms while rents rise. Every year that goes by, your payment stays flat and your equity compounds.

6. **Learn from both Dave Ramsey and the Rockefellers.**

Ramsey teaches financial discipline; the Rockefellers mastered financial multiplication. Combine both, and you have the mindset of a wealth builder.

7. **Leverage without education is a loaded weapon.**

Know your numbers. Run your Analyzer. Never borrow blind. The goal is not more debt — it's more freedom.

8. **Equity is lazy unless it's working.**

Refinance strategically, redeploy capital, and let your assets buy your next assets.

9. **The endgame: financial freedom and legacy.**

Leverage responsibly today so your family inherits not just properties — but a system for creating and sustaining wealth for generations.

FINAL REFLECTION

There's one more takeaway we haven't talked about enough—and it may be the most important one of all: **time**.

Some of you have seen the movie *Creed*. There's a scene where Rocky Balboa looks at Adonis and says, *"Time takes everybody out. Time is undefeated."* That line stuck with me because it's the truth. Markets change. Properties can be refinanced. Money can be lost and rebuilt. But time? You never get it back.

Time is the most valuable asset you own. Yet most people give away their best years trading hours for a paycheck—nine to five, five days a week—hoping that one day, maybe at sixty-seven, they'll finally get to enjoy life. That's the script we were handed. Work longer. Save harder. Wait patiently. Hope nothing goes wrong. I rejected that deal.

When you build cash-flowing assets, you're not just building wealth—you're buying back your time. You're creating optionality. You're giving yourself the ability to choose how you spend your days, who you spend them with, and what you work on—if you choose to work at all.

This skill set—learning how to analyze deals, use leverage responsibly, refinance intelligently, and reinvest consistently—isn't about becoming rich for the sake of it. It's about **taking control of your calendar**. It's about refusing to waste your most productive, energetic years stuck in a system that rewards patience over initiative.

Time is undefeated—but you can decide how you play the game. Build assets early. Let them work while you sleep. And don't wait until the clock runs out to start living.

I share this lesson with humility because I lived the conservative approach first. Paying off one property works, but it pales next to what calculated leverage can do. If you buy right, manage well, and respect the math, refinancing to scale is how you turn a single roof into a portfolio—and a paycheck into a legacy.

Financing determines speed, but operations determine survival. In the next chapter, we move into deal flow, management, and systems—the difference between owning property and running a real estate business.

CHAPTER 5
FINDING, EVALUATING & OPERATING PROPERTIES

Once financing stopped being my primary obstacle, I ran headfirst into the next reality: good deals are not evenly distributed. They don't show up neatly packaged. They don't wait patiently. And they rarely announce themselves loudly.

Early on, I made the mistake most beginners make. I relied too heavily on listing platforms. If something looked good online, I chased it. If it didn't, I ignored it. What I didn't understand was that by the time a deal looks obvious online, it's usually already overpriced.

Professionals don't wait for deals to be advertised. They build proximity to opportunity.

In my early years, I tried the "one real estate broker" approach. (A real estate broker does the same job as an agent but is licensed to work independently, and may employ agents. I'm using the terms interchangeably.) It felt tidy and safe: one person representing my interests, shopping me opportunities. But this is real estate, not a fairy tale. At the end of the day, realtors get paid on commission, and commission splits change behavior.

Here is my overview of an agent and a broker, so you know the difference:

A **real estate agent** is a licensed professional who represents buyers, sellers, or investors in property transactions. Agents are the boots on the ground. They tour properties, negotiate offers, gather comps, and help you navigate the process from contract to closing. When I first started investing, my agent was my secret weapon. I told him exactly what I was looking for: multi-family properties with value-add potential in solid rental areas. He knew my numbers, understood my criteria, and called me first when a deal hit the market. A good agent doesn't just open doors; they open opportunities.

A **broker** is a step above an agent—someone with additional licensing who can operate independently, manage agents, and often structure more complex transactions. In many states, every real estate office must have a managing broker who oversees the agents and ensures legal compliance. For investors, brokers are often the bridge to off-market deals, commercial listings, and creative financing opportunities. They're also typically the ones who can run deeper analyses or connect you with lenders, appraisers, and property managers. As I scaled my portfolio, I built a strong relationship with a broker who specialized in multi-family investments. He wasn't just sending MLS listings. He was analyzing cap rates, reviewing T-12 statements, and helping me negotiate seller-financing terms. That relationship led to one of my best deals: a six-unit property I bought below market because my broker knew the seller's situation and structured a win-win deal.

Here's the quiet truth most won't say out loud: when there are two close offers on the table—one brought by the listing agent and the other brought by an outside agent—there's often a gravitational pull toward the deal where the listing agent keeps the full commission. You can argue about how it *should* work; I'm telling you how it often *does* work in the field.

That's when I stopped playing telephone and went straight to listing brokers. Brokers know things before the market does:

- Why a seller is actually selling
- Whether price or terms matter more
- Which deals are about to quietly surface

I made it a habit to call brokers directly and say, very clearly, "Here's what I buy. Here's how I analyze. And here's how I close."

Credibility compounds faster than capital.

WHERE THE BEST DEALS COME FROM

- **Listing Brokers** – They are the easiest to close.
- **Relationship Brokers** – You can't have too many; give them guidelines so they don't waste your time. Quick "no" when not interested, lightning "yes" when it works.
- **Property Managers** – They know tired landlords before brokers do.
- **Lenders/Workout Officers** – They see stress first.
- **Wholesalers** – Some are good; some are bad. Vet them.
- **Public Records** – Tax liens, probates, code violations.
- **Driving for Dollars** – Roof tar patches, broken mailboxes, overgrown grass means tired owners.
- **Direct-to-Owner** – Letters, phone calls, respectful pitches.

When finding a deal, there is a lot of work to get to the close. The math of deal flow surprised me at first:

- Review ~20 properties
- Make ~6 offers
- Close ~1 deal

That ratio never bothered me once I understood it. Filtering is success, not failure. When a property passed the first glance, that's when I started my diligent work. I walked units myself. I reviewed systems personally. I verified rent rolls and expenses independently.

My golden rule is that the property has to meet 100% of my criteria or I pass. And remember my rules from chapter 1:

PARAMETER	CONDITIONS
Type of property	Multi-family, ideally 6–35 units.
Location	Within driving distance, in neighborhoods where rents were stable.
Rent-to-Price Ratio	Monthly rent had to equal at least 1% of the purchase price.
Condition	Livable but with room for improvement. No gut rehabs.
Financing	Fixed-rate mortgage only. No gimmicks.
Cash Flow	Positive from day one. No exceptions

If a deal is only 98% of my criteria, I don't do it. Half-baked deals turn into full-blown problems. My wife reminds me all the time: Another deal will knock in a few weeks. She's right. Saying no is a superpower. But when it is a yes, I move fast.

Here's what "fast" looks like:

1. Broker calls me with a property summary.
2. I run the numbers immediately through my Analyzer.
3. If it fits, I'm at the property within an hour.
4. We walk the building and peek at units.
5. While the broker grabs a slice of pizza across the street, I sit in my truck, open my laptop, and hammer through comps, rent rolls, and tax data.
6. Within fifteen minutes, I send an offer contingent on inspections, clean title, and environmental contingencies.

That speed, combined with credibility, is what wins.

DUE DILIGENCE: TRUST, BUT VERIFY

Due diligence is where investors are separated permanently.

This phase is uncomfortable because it forces confrontation—with sellers, contractors, tenants, and sometimes your own assumptions. Paper numbers mean nothing if physical reality contradicts them.

- **Reality vs. Projection**: A training twelve-month (T-12) scrub cuts through the fluff of pro forma (or formality) numbers, which are designed to make a property look good.
- **Expense Accuracy**: Scrubbing ensures you account for everything. Sellers often forget certain recurring costs (like landscaping, snow removal, or management fees).
- **True NOI (Net Operating Income)**: A proper scrub gives you the *real* NOI, which is the foundation for valuing income properties.

One deal stands out. After investing for a decade, I ran across my best deal yet. The seller lived abroad. His parents had passed away. The property was inherited, under-managed, and draining him emotionally. He didn't know the asset, didn't want to deal with tenants, and just wanted cash.

- My offer: $2.1 million
- True value: $3.2 million
- Close: 60 days
- Immediate equity: ~$1.1 million
- Cap Rate (Net Operating Income ÷ Purchase Price): 12% (. It measures return on a property as if you bought it all-cash. Higher is better, but too high often signals risk. Twelve percent is rare but possible when you find a distressed seller and act fast.)

On top of that, I ordered a cost segregation study (a tax strategy that accelerates depreciation) These can take a couple months.

Finally, I did my due diligence and hired some contractors to do a thorough inspection. I recommend not using a general inspector but using individual tradesmen (electrician, roofer, plumber, HVAC repairman, and a framer or mason (for structural integrity) to look over the property. A missed boiler or hidden oil tank can wipe out six figures in value. These aren't just inspectors. They're the people who will *fix it* if it's broken. And because I pay them fast, they always show up. That loyalty is worth more than any inspection checklist. Here are some things they need to look for:

- **Electrician** – panels, service size, wiring, and code hazards.
- **Roofer** – slope, flashing, penetrations, drainage, warranties.
- **Plumber/HVAC** – supply lines, sewer main (camera scoped), water heaters, shutoffs.
- **Framer/Mason** (as needed) – structural integrity.

Take photos of every model and serial number for mechanicals. Ask your trades: "If this fails in year one, what's most likely and how much would it cost?" I ran the numbers through my Analyzer to strip away the emotion of granite counters or fresh paint and focuses only on the facts:

- **Rent Roll**: Real rents, not broker promises.
- **Vacancy/Credit Loss**: 5–8% depending on market.
- **T-12 Scrub**: I rebuild expenses from trailing 12 months, not pro forma.
- **NOI**: Rebuilt bottom-up.
- **Metrics tested**: Cap Rate, Cash-on-Cash, DSCR.
- **Reserves**: Roofs, boilers, paving, not ignored.

Say the seller's pro forma shows the expenses are $45,000 a year. But when you scrub the T-12, you find:

- Utilities: $18,000
- Repairs: $15,000
- Insurance: $7,500
- Miscellaneous: $5,500
- **Total actual expenses = $46,000**

That's already $1,000 higher than what was advertised—and that difference impacts your cap rate, cash flow, and ultimately the property's value. Bottom line: A T-12 Scrub is like running a property through a lie detector test. You're not accepting what the seller tells you—you're rebuilding the financial truth.

A T-12 Scrub is like running a property through a lie detector test.

This is also where negotiation becomes nuanced. Sometimes the win isn't price—it's credits, timing, or scope. Sophisticated deals are rarely one-dimensional. That deal paid me in multiple ways: equity, cash flow, and tax savings.

SECTION 8 IS STABLE

While some landlords avoid government subsidized housing because of the annual inspections, I leaned in. In fact, about 40% of my portfolio is Section 8—and I've never once had to evict a Section 8 tenant. When handled properly, it can provide reliable payments, long-term tenancy, and reduced vacancy.

During COVID, when private-market tenants struggled and eviction moratoriums tied landlords' hands, my Section 8 checks arrived like clockwork on the first of the month. That stability was a lifeline. Yes, I had tenants who fell behind on their portion of the rent, and it was stressful not being able to take action. The governor had banned evictions, but my mortgage payments didn't stop. I used to shake my head and think: If I can't walk into a grocery store and grab food for free, why am I being forced to provide housing for free?

Eventually, the state rolled out a Temporary Rental Assistance program. I personally helped tenants fill out the forms. Two weeks later, I received a massive check that caught everyone up in one shot. It wasn't luck—it was strategy and relationships. That's why I say Section 8, if managed right, is one of the most stable pieces of my portfolio.

Some of my Section 8 tenants have been with me for over twenty-five years. They pay their portion, they stay put, and they value the stability just as much as I do. Once a tenant gets Section 8, they rarely want to leave. And here's the kicker: if they fail to pay their portion or are evicted for cause, they risk losing their benefits *for life*. That creates built-in accountability.

I once bought a six-unit garden-style building at a steep discount because the seller wanted out. The problem? Apartment #1 was occupied by the local drug dealer—"Big Momma," a woman in her seventies who ran the neighborhood trade.

She was on Section 8, so I had leverage. I showed up with a buddy of mine who was a police officer and had him sit in the driveway with his patrol car. I was straight with Big Momma. I told her, "You have a choice. I can let this officer park here until you get arrested, which will cost you your Section 8 benefits for life, or you can pack up and leave in seven days."

She looked me dead in the eye, gave a half-smile, and said: "Oh, Mr. Glenn, you don't play. I'll leave."

And she did. The building stabilized, my tenants were happier, and I was holding a property I had picked up for a steal—all because I understood the system and wasn't afraid to enforce it.

Most of the resistance comes down to inspections and rent ceilings. Some landlords don't like being told what to fix or how much they can charge. But I see inspections as a benefit, not a burden. They keep the property in check, and if the tenant causes damage, Section 8 enforces accountability on them.

As for rents, my approach is balanced. I keep a mix of market-rate and Section 8 units, which gives me both stability and flexibility

KEY BENEFITS OF SECTION 8

- **Predictable Inspections** – If you maintain your properties, you'll pass without issues.
- **Guaranteed Payments** – The government's portion arrives on time, every time—even during crises.
- **Tenant Accountability** – If tenants fail to pay their share, they can lose their benefits permanently.
- **Low Turnover** – Once in, most Section 8 tenants stay for years, reducing vacancy costs.

By treating the Section 8 office as a partner, not a hurdle, I built strong relationships that consistently send me reliable tenants. While other landlords avoided the program, I leaned in. For me, Section 8 has meant fewer headaches, more stability, and a portfolio that weathers storms—even once-in-a-lifetime ones like COVID.

SECURITY

One of the smartest investments I ever made was in lighting and cameras.

One morning, George, my super at an eighteen-unit building I owned, called me: "Glenn, there's blood in the front hallway."

I had installed bright LED hallway lights and cameras, so I told him, "Go to the maintenance room and rewind the video."

What we saw was surreal: a domestic dispute had spilled into the hall. A tenant named Sara tried to escape her boyfriend. As the door was closing, her boyfriend had momentum from chasing her and ran into the door and slammed it closed; her hand didn't clear the frame, and her finger was severed instantly. The video showed her boyfriend scrambling, eventually putting the finger into a Chicken McNugget box before rushing her to the emergency room.

The next day, I got a call from a malpractice lawyer claiming my hydraulic door closer was defective. I calmly sent him the video. Within hours, he called back and said, "I'm sorry for wasting your time."

That one small investment in security equipment saved me from a lawsuit and months of legal headaches. Cameras and lighting don't just deter crime; they protect you, your tenants, and your investment.

TENANT MANAGEMENT 101

Tenant management isn't complicated—but it is unforgiving. My standard has always been not to rent a unit I wouldn't live in myself.

Every time I walk my properties, I step into a tenant's shoes. I use my nose before I use my eyes. Does the hall smell like old carpet or mop water? Does a stair tread wobble? Do the boiler gauges read normally? Properties "talk" if you pay attention.

And when a unit turns over, I ask one question: *Could my family move in today?*

If the answer isn't a confident yes, then it's not ready.

I've learned that small touches matter: bright lighting, fresh caulk lines, sharp outlet covers, blinds that open and close smoothly. These small things don't just make the place presentable. They tell tenants that the property is cared for. Care reduces turnover more than any rent discount ever will.

Communication

Tenants don't need you to be perfect. They need you to be accessible and predictable. When they need some work done, you need to let them know you heard them, even if you can't get to it immediately. Here are some rules I go by regarding communication:

- Acknowledge the request the same day. Even if the fix will take a week, respond within twenty-four hours.

- Be specific. "Maria, Antonio will arrive at 9:30 a.m. with the part."
- Close the loop. Always follow up: "All set? Anything else while we're here?"

Speed and clarity build trust. And trust builds long-term tenants. Consistency matters more than flexibility. The same rule applies to everyone. Exceptions create resentment and chaos. That principle sets the tone for everything else.

Screening Tenants

Tenants are not problems to be managed; they are relationships to be structured.

One subtle but powerful way to build and maintain relationships is to play the role of property manager. I never let them know I'm the owner. This creates a buffer. Policies aren't "Glenn's rules"—they're company standards. Rent due dates, late fees, and hall clutter—all become professional guidelines rather than personal battles.

Behind the scenes, each property is owned by its own LLC, which signs a management agreement with my management company. This isn't just legal protection; it's professionalism. And professionalism builds tenant trust.

As the property manager, I am firm but fair. I set clear expectations, which prevents 90% of conflict. And screening is non-negotiable:

- Income verification
- Background checks
- Rental history

Being "nice" at this stage is expensive later. Applications, credit checks, pay stubs—all important. But they don't tell the whole story. That's why I use the car test.

After meeting an applicant, I walk them back to their car. If it looks like a landfill, I know how they'll treat my unit. If it's neat and cared for, odds are the apartment will be too. It's not science, but it's been uncannily accurate over decades.

Setting and Collecting Rent

Setting and collecting rent can be tricky. One way to avoid shorting yourself is to never guess on rent. I triangulate by researching three sources to find out comparable rents in the area. I look at the following:

- **Online comps**: I look at renting sites such as Zillow and Apartments.com for comparable rents based on the number of beds and baths, and finishes.
- **Rentometer:** This is a paid online tool for landlords, investors, and property managers that provides quick rent estimates by comparing a property's rent to similar rentals in the same area.
- **HUD FMRs (Fair Market Rents):** These are annual estimates by the U.S. Department of Housing and Urban Development used mainly to set payment standards for housing assistance programs like the Housing Choice Voucher (Section 8). It lets me see where Section 8 sits in each town.

I aim for the middle: never the cheapest, never the most expensive. Fair, clean, well-kept units rent in days, not weeks.

Collections: Grace with Boundaries

Life happens. A job loss, reduced hours, or a medical bill can throw a tenant off. My rule is structured compassion:

- Friendly reminder after the due date.
- If they're proactive, we draft a short, written plan.
- Stick to the plan—no exceptions.
- I've had tenants hit rough patches, recover, and stay for years

—some even referring friends to me because they knew I treated them fairly.

- Court is always my last resort, not my first.

Maintenance

The biggest thing I can say about maintenance is to have a fierce work ethic. If a water heater broke on Christmas Eve (and yes, that actually happened), I didn't complain; I fixed it. That's what it took, and that's what I was willing to do. Real estate doesn't care about your calendar. Tenants don't care that it's a holiday. Problems show up when they show up, and the people who win are the ones who show up too.

My wife and I shared not only a vision, but also a work ethic that matched. That alignment made all the difference. We didn't sit around waiting for opportunities to fall into our laps. We chased them, managed them, and handled every challenge head-on. If she needed to manage the books while I was on site repairing something, we did it without question. If it meant late nights reviewing leases or early mornings meeting contractors before work, we made it happen. Together, we built a rhythm where sacrifice wasn't a burden. It was an investment in our future.

Work ethic is often overlooked in conversations about wealth. People want to talk about tax strategies, financing hacks, or negotiation tactics. While those things matter, all the strategy in the world is worthless if you're not willing to put in the effort when it counts. The truth is, most people aren't willing to do what it takes consistently. They'll work hard for a season but not year after year. They'll fix one problem, but not the tenth in a row. That's where the difference is made.

Wealth isn't built on big flashy wins. It's built on small, unglamorous actions repeated with discipline. Every time I crawled into a cold basement to check a leaking pipe, every time I took a call at midnight from a tenant, every time we gave up comfort for progress, we were laying bricks in the foundation of financial freedom. That's the lesson I want to pass on: wealth follows work ethic. Without it, you're just chasing shortcuts that don't exist.

One way to prevent having to make repairs in the middle of the night or during holidays is to make it a priority to be consistent with preventive maintenance. Early on, I made a rookie mistake: I skipped preseason boiler servicing because "it ran fine last year." At 2:17 a.m. on a freezing January night, my phone rang. Half the building had lost heat. I scrambled with space heaters, apologetic texts, and a plumber billing me emergency rates.

Wealth isn't built on big flashy wins. It's built on small, unglamorous actions repeated with discipline

---

That night cost me thousands. But the higher cost was my reputation.

From then on, I adopted a new system: service before season. We bleed baseboards, check safeties, test thermostats, and swap weak parts before the first frost. It costs a little up front, but it saves tenfold in panic calls and sleepless nights.

TOOLKIT – TENANT MANAGEMENT ESSENTIALS

Before Move-In:

- Inspect with tenant, take photos, sign condition form.
- Deliver a welcome packet (contacts, trash policy, maintenance process).
- Require 1.5 months' rent security deposit + first month upfront.

Screening:

- Require a credit score ≥ 640.
- Verify employment (two pay stubs).
- Perform the car test.

- Check references personally.

Section 8 Prep:

- Use GFCIs (ground fault receptacle interrupter) in kitchen and bathrooms.
- Install handrails, smoke/CO detectors, self-closing front door
- Check fire extinguishers and make sure any egress is clear.
- Fix issues proactively; pass inspection on first try.

Ongoing Management:

- Provide bright lighting, clean common areas, visible signage.
- Install cameras in entrances and halls.
- Service boilers/furnaces before season.
- Same-day acknowledgment of all issues.

WORKING WITH SUBCONTRACTORS

If real estate is a long game, then subcontractors are your teammates in the late innings—the ones you call when the game's tight and one mistake can flip the score. Over the years, I learned the most valuable skill isn't swinging the hammer myself—it's listening. Listening to the person who's been soldering copper since before I graduated college. Listening to the roofer who can hear a soft spot with his boots. Listening to the electrician who knows why the breaker keeps tripping, even though the panel looks fine.

When I first started, if something broke, I fixed it. Money was tight, and I was proud. I was handy enough to be dangerous. Some days I did great. Other days, I'd spend Saturday "saving" three hundred dollars and Sunday paying a pro six hundred to undo what I did. Those were tuition days. They taught me where my strengths end and where someone else's begin.

My wife's been telling me for years: "Enjoy what you've built. Let others do the work." I try. I really do. But I'm still the guy who will change a water heater or swap a zone valve if it means a tenant has hot water by dinner. My electrician laughs: "You're the only millionaire I know who still pulls out the pro-press." I tell him the same thing every time: "That's one of the reasons I became a millionaire." Not because I do every task, but because I care about outcomes, and I know enough to hold everyone—me included—to a high standard.

Subcontractors can protect your margins or destroy them quietly.

People ask how to find great subs. Here's the truth: you earn them. Pay fast. Decide fast. Be organized. Don't shop every bid to death. Don't weaponize "my cousin can do it cheaper." Handle scope changes like a pro. Share credit for a job well done.

When the work is done and clean, I cut the check. Often the same day. Sometimes I drive it over. Subcontractors remember who pays them first. They'll answer your call at 7 a.m. when someone else goes to voicemail. They'll squeeze you in on Friday when the schedule is packed. They'll send their best guy to your job instead of the trainee.

When something blows up, I try to be the calmest voice on the line. I will say, "Here's the address. The shutoff is in the basement. The tenant's name is Sarah. She's home and her number is.... Send me a picture when you find the issue." The clearer I am, the faster they move. When it's done, I thank them, pay them, and send a recap so we both remember what happened at 11:42 p.m. three months from now.

One Christmas Eve a supply line under a vanity popped. The plumber on call drove over, swapped the line, dried the cabinet, and asked if we wanted to proactively replace the other two lines in the unit while he was there. I told him to do it. We paid the emergency rate and a little extra as a thank-you. The tenant texted: "You saved our Christmas." That plumber has never turned me down since.

A roofer once told me, "I price on headache and history. You're low on both." That's the discount you want—based on trust not haggling.

Great subs attract each other. Your best plumber knows a great electrician. Your electrician knows a roofer you'll keep for a decade. Before long, you have an A Team that knows your standards so well you spend more time approving work than explaining it.

I once asked my electrician why he referred a particular HVAC tech to me. He smiled and said, "He cares like you do. He doesn't just fix the thing; he fixes the reason." That's the kind of sub I want.

Even now, I'll still do small things: label a panel, mount a CO detector, change a filter, replace a leaky supply line at 8 p.m. It's not about saving fifty bucks. It's about staying close to the reality inside the walls. When you lose touch with the physical building, your expectations drift and your budgets turn into fiction.

I don't do it because I have to. I do it because it keeps me honest. It also tells my team, tenants, and subs that I'm not the owner who points and disappears. I'm present. That presence buys a kind of respect you can't demand, and it builds relationships so when emergencies happen, and they will, you can respond to them efficiently.

One time a third-floor tub in a four-family unit kept leaking into the kitchen below. I swapped the trap twice, but it still leaked. Finally, my plumber crawled in, stared for a minute, and said, "It's not the trap. It's the overflow gasket. It's dried out, and the tub flexes." Thirty minutes later it was fixed. I had spent two weekends and three trips to the store all to avoid the forty-dollar truth. Another time, I had a leak from the third floor to the second, and neither of us could figure it out. Determined, I brought a towel and a bathing suit, jumped into the shower, and told him, "We're going to solve this today." He laughed his head off while I splashed around, convinced it was the drainpipe. I was wrong again. After more poking around, we found the real culprit: a rusted-out galvanized pipe hidden in the wall with a hole right on the straight run. Sometimes it takes both of us—one with a wrench, the other in swim trunks—to finally solve the problem.

The lesson? The obvious answer isn't always the right one, and pride will cost you more than humility. I could have sworn it was the drain. I was sure of it. But my plumber's patience and experience uncovered the real issue. That's when I realized the cheapest fix is often the one you can't see—and that having another set of eyes (and ears) on a problem saves time, money, and headaches. Real estate isn't about knowing everything yourself; it's about knowing when to trust the people who do.

Another time, an electrician told me a panel "looked tired." That's not a technical term, and I almost ignored it. He ran his hand along the breakers, pointed to heat discoloration I wouldn't have noticed, and explained why a loose neutral was about to become an expensive surprise. We replaced it on a Wednesday afternoon instead of on a Saturday at 9 p.m. with tenants in the dark. That's when I really started listening, not just nodding but listening.

Here's the quiet rule I live by now: if the tradesperson can explain the "why," and it makes sense, I back them. Nine times out of ten, their path is cheaper over the life of the building than my "save a buck today" impulse.

Your A Team isn't built in a day. It's built through standards, repetition, and accountability. But not everyone stays on the roster forever. Sometimes it's quality. Sometimes it's communication. Sometimes it's attitude. I don't burn bridges, but I don't keep building on a shaky one either.

If I see a pattern—missed windows without a call, sloppy cleanup, "that's good enough" vibes—I sit down and talk it through once. If it doesn't change, I say thanks and move on. The bar is simple: treat my buildings and my tenants like you'd want your mother's place treated. If that doesn't resonate, we're not a match.

Scope, Change, and the Art of No Surprises

When I award a job, I do a scope walk. Not a thirty-second "here's the bathroom" job. We walk, we point, we talk about the end state. I ask them how they'd do it. I shut up and listen. I'm not looking for the cheapest way; I'm looking for the right way that won't get me another call in six months.

A roofer once looked at a soft spot and said, "We can patch it." He noticed my hesitation. "Or," he added, "we can pull the decking and do ice shield up three feet." That's what we did. Ten years later, it still hasn't leaked. The patch would have been cheaper but I would have had to do it at least twice.

On my walkthroughs, I also set non-negotiables: protect the hall floors, contain the dust, finish the edges like they'll be photographed, and leave it cleaner than you found it. We discuss the tenant impact. We pick times that respect mornings, nights, and nap times. When workers treat a home like a home, tenants stay longer and complain less.

I've learned that subs hate surprises as much as owners do. A clear scope prevents "Oh, I thought you wanted…" conversations.

It's simple language:

- What we're doing – "Replace kitchen shutoffs and angle stops; no PEX visible."
- How it should end up – "Wall patched flush, bead tight, match texture, paint to logical break."
- What's included – "Haul debris off site; supply Delta cartridges if discovered."
- What's not – Anything behind walls beyond the immediate cabinet bay unless approved.

When the scope is crystal clear—"Install six new fixtures of the same model, replace valves, patch and paint to break"—I like a fixed bid. It aligns incentives and kills nickel-and-diming. When the job is exploratory—"Find the leak we can't see that only happens in wind from the east"—I'll like to use a time and materials (T&M) bid with a not-to-exceed number. I want the tech curious, not defensive. The key is trust. (T&M works only with subs who treat your money like their own.)

A contractor once told me: "If you force me to guess all the unknowns in a fixed price, I'll price the job like the worst case. If you give me room to think, it'll often cost you less." He was right.

When something does change—and it will—we treat it like a mini-contract: "Add: replace corroded galvanized with copper from riser to tee; + $180; schedule impact: + 2 hours." No drama, just clarity. I sign it. They proceed. We both sleep.

How you treat subcontractors is how your buildings will be treated. If you nickel-and-dime, you get corners cut. If you delay payment, you get late arrivals and the B crew. If you communicate like a grown-up and pay like clockwork, you get people who answer your call on holidays and care about your tenants like they're their own.

My kids will inherit the properties one day. But they'll also inherit something invisible: a culture. A network of people who know the standard, respect the process, and trust the family behind it. That's worth as much as the deeds in the safe.

Subcontractor Commandments

- **Listen first.** If they can explain the why, and it holds water, back them.
- **Standardize.** Have one right faucet, one right paint, and one right lockset. Speed lives in sameness.
- **Clarify Scope.** Make sure everyone knows the desired end state.
- **Handle changes like adults.** Write it down, sign it, move on.
- **Pay fast.** This is the cheapest leverage you own.
- **Protect homes.** Drop cloths, dust control, finished edges, clean hallways.
- **Permit what needs permitting.** Sleep at night; pass inspection once.
- **Check the punch.** That last five percent is what people remember.

- **Be calm in emergencies.** Give the subs clear info, a clear plan, and clear gratitude.
- **Upgrade the roster when needed. Be** kind and firm, then move onward.

Follow those, and you'll never be the owner frantically dialing through a contact list while the ceiling drips. You'll be the owner whose phone gets answered on the first ring.

Standardization: The Quiet Force Multiplier

When you close on your first building, you expect excitement. What you don't expect is seller to drop in your hand a giant, jingling key ring with a hundred mismatched keys, sharp edges digging into your palm, none labeled, none making sense. You don't expect to stand there wondering *Which one even opens the front door?*

That is when it clicked for me: chaos costs money. Efficiency creates freedom. And the path to efficiency is standardization.

At first, I lived with the chaos. I'd drive across town for a simple repair, spend ten minutes testing keys, and sometimes still have to call the tenant down to let me in. When contractors came—pest control, the plumber, the electrician—I'd either have to meet them personally or hand them a random key and hope it worked. Then I bit the bullet and developed a master key system. One master lock setup across all properties. Every tenant got fresh locks on move-in, but my one master key could open every door across my portfolio. Suddenly, my world changed. No more "100 key" ring. No more guessing. No more wasted time.

But that simplicity came with a decision—and a cost. You can go the cheap route and buy standard Lowe's or Home Depot Kwikset locks for $50–$60 each, or you can spend a little more and install a lock system tied into a true master-key setup. I chose the latter, and I've never looked back.

The benefits go far beyond convenience. My plumber and electrician both have a master key—and I trust them. That means if something comes up, I can send them directly to the building without being there. They can access the front door, the tenant's unit, the boiler room—everything they need—without delays, coordination headaches, or emergency calls pulling me away from my day.

I also installed Knox Boxes on the exterior of my buildings. The fire chief loves me for it. In the rare event of a fire or emergency, there's one secure key available immediately. No doors kicked in. No wasted minutes. No unnecessary damage. When seconds matter, access matters.

This is one of those upgrades that feels small but pays dividends every single year—in time saved, stress reduced, and emergencies handled properly. It's not just about locks. It's about control, efficiency, and running your properties like a professional, not a hobbyist.

The ripple effects were huge. Pest control could sweep a building without knocking on every door. My plumber could handle emergencies when I was out of town. My electrician didn't waste twenty minutes waiting in the rain. Everyone on my team had the same single key.

That small investment paid me back thousands of times over in time saved, stress reduced, and credibility earned with tenants. It also taught me something bigger: standardization isn't a luxury; it's survival if you want to scale.

I'll never forget standing in the aisle at a big box store, staring at a wall of faucets, trying to decide: chrome, brushed nickel, $39 specials, $189 high-end pieces. Early on, I always picked the cheapest. A faucet is a faucet, right? Wrong.

Standardization is essential for scale

What happened was a nightmare. Every unit had a different faucet, a different cartridge, and different stems. My plumbers carried around a parts museum. If a faucet broke, we'd waste hours tracking down replacement parts. Sometimes they weren't even made anymore. Tenants were frustrated. Repairs cost more.

That's when I chose one brand: Delta, and Delta only. It wasn't the cheapest up front, but it was the cheapest in the long run. Now every sink, every tub, every shower diverter matches. My subs know them by heart. I stock spare cartridges. Repairs went from chaotic to seamless. Because I keep the same parts on hand, I can repair on the spot without running to the store or buying something new. The job gets done in minutes, not hours.

Don't save $15 today if it costs you $500 tomorrow.

Every unit of mine now has power-flush toilets. They use a fraction of the water, and they almost never clog. It's not glamorous, but it's one of the smartest standardization moves I've ever made. That one choice has saved me from countless calls from angry tenants.

Sometimes wealth is built not just by what you add, but by what you avoid. At one point, my storage room looked like a paint recycling center—thirty-five half-used cans of off-white. Every time we opened a wall or did a turnover, we'd have to guess the shade. Half the time, the touch-up dried two shades darker, and we'd have to repaint the whole wall anyway. That's when I switched to two colors only: one for walls, one for trim. Same brand, same sheen, same code. Every single unit. Now my crews don't waste time guessing. When a wall gets opened, it's patched, painted, and perfect. Tenants never even notice the repair. It sounds simple. But across dozens of units, that consistency saves thousands of dollars and hours every year.

Regarding flooring, I've lived through it all: carpet smells, tile grout crumbles, and hardwood scratches. Every turnover meant a new headache. Then I found my solution: water-resistant, click-lock laminate. It's durable, attractive, and uniform across every property. Now, every turnover is predictable. My crews know how to lay it. I stock the same SKU (stock keeping unit) in bulk. Tenants love the clean look, and I don't deal with the endless carpet cleaning bills or tile repairs.

Consistency doesn't just save money; it creates a better tenant experience.

Regarding ceiling fans. Tenants don't clean them, and eventually the dust splatters across freshly painted ceilings. The result? A ceiling that looks like it's been neglected for years, even if you just invested time and money to keep it pristine.

Now, when tenants move out, I always repaint the ceilings as part of turnover, and I remove the ceiling fans. It's not that I dislike ceiling fans themselves. They serve a purpose, especially for air circulation. But the ripple effect of poor upkeep outweighs the benefit. For me, standardization and systemization are everything. If I can eliminate one more variable that leads to maintenance headaches, repainting costs, or tenant complaints, I will.

Banning ceiling fans became part of my standardization philosophy as a landlord. Standardization is not just about what you choose to install; it's also about what you choose *not* to install. Every property decision should reduce long-term costs, simplify turnover, and create consistency across your portfolio. Ceiling fans don't pass that test.

Instead, I stick with durable, low-maintenance fixtures that don't rely on tenant upkeep. Lighting should be simple, modern, and easy to replace. Ventilation should come from reliable systems that I can maintain on my schedule, not tenants' timetable. By setting the standard and enforcing it, I reduce variables, eliminate repeat problems, and protect the quality of my properties.

The bigger lesson? Don't just think about how something looks the day you buy or install it. Think about the next five or ten years, and whether tenants will care for it the way you need them to. Spoiler: most won't. Build your systems for reality, not theory.

Kitchens sell apartments—period. Every unit I own includes a full appliance package: stove, microwave, refrigerator, and dishwasher. But the real surprise is the countertops. Most landlords assume granite is too expensive for rentals. I thought so too until I struck a deal with a local granite supplier. I told them I'd take whatever remnants they had on hand, any color they could cut that week. Because of that arrangement, I now get a granite sink installed for less than the cost of Formica. I've standardized all my units. Tenants love it, it photographs beautifully, and it actually costs me less. It's a win-win that elevates the look and feel of my units while keeping expenses down.

Garbage disposals might sound like an upgrade, but in rentals, they're nothing but trouble. Clogs, jams, and maintenance calls eat into your time and profit. I don't include them in any of my apartments. Trust me, you'll thank me later for skipping them.

I pay attention to all the details. I assess everything outside, from drainage to lawn maintenance, because all of my properties are long-term investments.

First, I check if basements are taking on water or moisture. If so, I make sure all downspouts drain away from the building and that the grading is pitched properly. If not, I fix it first, extending piping far from the building, using underground drains with stone and a discharge emitter.

Next, I inspect foundations for cracks. If I continue to see water inside, I'll cut to the chase: I find the lowest point in the basement and add a seepage pit and sump pump about three to four feet below the slab, pumping water out into my lateral drains.

Landscaping also matters. I look for efficiency, not Instagram aesthetics. Rocks that block mowers get removed. Excess plants, shrubs, and trees come out. Some "green" enthusiasts may not like it, but I prioritize ease of maintenance for decades to come.

When everything goes according to plan, it's a beautiful thing. One of my favorite days was a turnover sprint. A market tenant gave thirty days' notice. We pre-ordered supplies, scheduled the painter for day one, the plumber for day two (new shutoffs and a Delta swap), and the flooring crew for day three. On day four, we hung blinds, installed new lights, and did a hotel-level clean. On day five, I took photos at noon, published the listing at 1 p.m., and had three qualified applicants by dinner. The new tenant moved in the following week. Five days vacant, full asking rent, and a unit I'd live in myself.

When a plan comes together like that, it's not luck. It's good planning and the quiet power of standardization, trusting your subs, and paying attention before the clock starts.

Standardization changed everything.

- Same locks.
- Same faucets.
- Same flooring.
- Same paint families.

At first glance, standardization seems like a landlord's trick to save money. And yes, it does. But the bigger picture is this: standardization creates systems.

When my kids inherit these properties, they won't have to guess which paint to use or which faucet to order. They'll inherit a machine that runs. One key, one faucet, one floor, one paint, one system. They won't be buried in chaos. They'll be able to grow what I've built, not just maintain it. That's the true purpose of standardization—not just saving time, but creating a business that lasts beyond one lifetime.

At some point, I stopped thinking like a property owner and started thinking like an operator. Owners react. Operators plan. Operating means:

- Documented systems
- Predictable outcomes
- Delegated responsibility

That shift didn't happen overnight. It happened deal by deal, problem by problem. And once it happened, growth became sustainable. At this point, most investors can operate profitably. But profit alone doesn't protect wealth.

In the next chapter, we move into the invisible layers—legal structure, insurance, and tax strategy. These are the systems you don't notice until you need them. And when you need them, nothing else matters.

CHAPTER 6
LLCS, INSURANCE & TAX OPTIMIZATION

Most people think about legal structure *after* something goes wrong. That's backward. Legal structure is not about avoiding responsibility—it's about containing risk so one mistake doesn't undo decades of work.

Early on, I learned to stop thinking like a property owner and start thinking like a business operator. Businesses don't own assets casually. They hold them intentionally, with clear boundaries.

That's why my rule became simple and firm: *One property. One LLC. No exceptions.*

LLCS

From the very beginning, I knew one thing: if I was going to build wealth, I had to protect it. My first deal wasn't just a building. It was a lesson in structure. I put the property into an LLC. An LLC (limited liability company) is a legal container. It holds the property, contracts, leases, and liabilities tied to that one asset.

At first, I kept the names simple. If the building sat on Tyler Avenue, I called it the Tyler Ave Realty Group, LLC. The next one was Jordan Place Realty, LLC. It was straightforward. Then I ran out of streets and got creative. A four-family down the block bBecame 4 Plex Realty, LLC. A six-unit Became 6 Plex Realty, LLC. Then came 8 Plex, 10 Plex, 12 Plex, 28 Plex —you get the idea. My kids still laugh: "Dad's going to end up with 100 Plex Realty, LLC."

An LLC is a firewall. When structured correctly, it prevents problems in one property from spreading to others—or to your personal life. This isn't theoretical. Tenants fall. Contractors make mistakes. Neighbors sue. Cities change rules. None of these events are rare. What matters is how much damage they can do.

If something goes wrong at 18 Tyler Avenue, the claim is against Tyler Ave Realty Group, LLC not against my personal house, my kids' college funds, or the assets in another building two towns away. That wall is how I sleep well at night.

I've heard every version of the counterargument:

- "I'll just put all ten properties in one LLC."
- "I'll use one holding LLC and DBA names for each building."
- "I'll keep it in my personal name and add extra insurance."

Every path looks cheaper until something happens. The problem with one bucket is that everything in the bucket is exposed if any one property gets sued. The problem with doing business as (DBA) an entity is that that entity is not a legal shield. It's a nickname for the same legal person. And the problem with keeping it in your personal name is obvious.

One LLC per property gives me clean risk isolation. If something goes wrong at 6 Plex Realty, 8 Plex is untouched. So is Tyler. So is my personal world. It also gives me clean bookkeeping, clean lending, and clean exits. If I ever sell, I can sell the real estate or, in some cases, sell the LLC membership interests (with counsel) without untangling a spiderweb of assets.

Years ago, a delivery guy slipped on fresh snow near a side entrance. We had salted, we had shoveled, and we had logs to prove it, but accidents are accidents. The injury claim came in against the property LLC. That was the only target. Not my home. Not the other buildings. Not the management company. The claim got handled by the insurance attached to that one LLC, and we moved on.

Same winter, a landlord I know—good guy—kept three buildings in his personal name to save fees. One night a tenant's guest fell down a dim stairwell. The claim reached everything he owned. He got through it, but it was a brutal wake-up call. He now has more LLCs than I do.

Setting up a single-property LLC isn't glamorous, but the steps matter. When you do it right, you earn the protection you think you have.

My rhythm looks like this:

1. Form the LLC before you sign the purchase contract (or at least before closing). I check name availability, file articles / certificate of formation with the state, and select myself as the registered agent.
2. Draft a simple operating agreement (even for a single-member LLC). It says who owns it, who manages it, and how decisions happen.
3. Get an EIN (Tax Identification Number) from the IRS (takes five minutes).
4. Open a business bank account in the LLC's name.
5. Make sure the purchase contract and deed list the LLC as buyer (or transfer carefully later with your attorney and lender's blessing).
6. Bind insurance in the LLC's name (property + general liability; often an umbrella on top).
7. Sign vendor contracts and leases in the LLC's name.
8. Keep books for that LLC separate, clean, and simple.

Clean books matter more than most people realize. Sloppy bookkeeping weakens protection. Organized records reinforce credibility with banks, attorneys, and insurers.

Municipal licenses, inspections, and naming consistency aren't bureaucratic nuisances. They're part of the system that keeps everything standing under pressure.

Structure doesn't eliminate risk. It limits blast radius.

REGISTERED AGENT

When you form an LLC, the law requires that you designate a registered agent. This is the individual or company officially responsible for receiving legal documents, government notices, tax forms, and service of process (such as lawsuits) on behalf of your business. Think of the registered agent as your LLC's official point of contact with the state. They must have a physical address (not a P.O. Box) in the state where your LLC is registered and be available during normal business hours. You can act as your own registered agent, but many business owners hire a professional service to keep their home address off public records, ensure an important notice is never missed, and provide consistency if you operate in multiple states. In short, a registered agent is not a business partner or manager. They are the legal mailbox for your company, making sure you don't miss deadlines or legal obligations that could put your LLC at risk.

INSURANCE

For years I treated property insurance as a check-the-box item—pay the premium, file the binder, and move on. Big mistake. Property insurance isn't just paperwork; it's the firewall that protects everything you've built. A single uncovered loss—a fire, a slip-and-fall, a burst pipe—can erase decades of work in an afternoon. If you own multiple properties, you're running a business, and insurance is a critical operating system.

1. Shop Every Year—No Exceptions

Complacency is expensive. Insurers count on renewals slipping through on autopilot with automatic rate hikes. I never let that happen. Each year, about ninety days before renewal, I have my broker rebid every policy. I want at least three quotes per building and a side-by-side comparison of coverages, deductibles, and endorsements. I create a spreadsheet listing policy numbers, expiration dates, premiums, and coverage amounts. Treat it like a lease-renewal calendar and never miss the shopping window.

2. Insure for Replacement Cost, Not Sentiment

The goal is to rebuild, not to win a popularity contest with your insurer. I don't chase inflated market values, and I never underinsure. I cover to the true replacement cost—what it would take to rebuild the structure today with current materials and labor, not yesterday's prices. Too low? A total loss leaves you funding the gap. Too high? You're just donating premium dollars to the carrier.

3. Always Require Renter's Insurance

Every lease I write requires tenants to carry renter's insurance and list my management company as an additional interest. This does two things:

1. Protects the tenant's personal belongings so they're not knocking on my door for a payout after a fire.
2. Provides liability coverage that kicks in before mine if the tenant causes damage (like that kitchen grease fire that started with a midnight snack). Verification is non-negotiable: proof of coverage before keys change hands and annual confirmation at renewal.

4. Separate Policies for Every LLC

Since each property sits inside its own LLC, each LLC has its own insurance policy. Period. Why? If a tenant sues one building, I don't want them reaching the assets of another. Segregating ownership and insurance is like watertight bulkheads on a ship: one leak won't sink the entire holdings.

5. Align Insurance with Your Trust

After transferring my deeds into a family trust, I had every carrier issue a rider listing the trust as an additional insured. Without that step, a claim could have been denied because the "named insured" no longer technically owned the property. One email to the broker fixed it and now every binder reads: *LLC Name & The Glenn Polansky Family Trust, Additional Insured.*

6. Coverage That Counts

A good policy for rentals should include:

- **Property/Building** – Covers the replacement cost on the structure.
- **Loss of Rents** – Covers the rent while repairs are made after a covered loss.
- **General Liability** – Covers at least $1 to $2M per occurrence.
- **Umbrella Policy** – An extra layer of liability (I carry $5M) that sits on top of the property and auto policies.
- **Equipment Breakdown** – Covers boilers, HVAC, and elevators.
- **Water Backup/Sump Overflow** – Covers sewer and drain, which is often excluded by default.

7. Work the Claim Like a Pro

When disaster strikes:

- Document everything with photos/video before touching a broom.
- Call your broker first, not just the 1-800 claim line.
- Get your own contractor estimates.
- Keep a log of every conversation—date, name, action item. A well-organized claim file saves time, stress, and thousands of dollars.

8. Annual "Insurance Audit" Checklist

- Verify that replacement-cost limits match today's building costs.
- Review deductibles vs. reserves. Raise deductibles to lower premiums only if cash reserves are strong.
- Confirm trust/LLC names and addresses are correct.
- Re-shop with at least three carriers.
- Require updated renter's insurance certificates from every tenant.
- Evaluate umbrella policy for net-worth growth.

A fellow investor friend of mine owned a mid-sized multi-family building in northern New Jersey. One winter, a freak electrical fire started in a vacant unit's wall cavity. By the time the fire department arrived, smoke and water damage had spread through half the building.

The direct fire damage was bad enough, but what really shocked him was the hidden financial fallout:

- **Tenant Relocation Costs** – Several families had to move out immediately. Without "loss of rents" coverage, he would have lost months of income.
- **Water Remediation & Mold Prevention** – Sprinkler and fire-hose water soaked everything. The remediation alone was a six-figure bill.
- **Code Upgrades** – When you rebuild after a loss, towns often require you to bring the entire building up to the latest code—electrical, plumbing, ADA access—even if only part of it burned.

Fortunately, my friend wasn't flying blind. He had insured the building for full replacement cost, not just market value. That distinction meant the carrier covered the true cost of rebuilding at today's construction prices—including those code upgrades. And he required every tenant to carry renter's insurance. Their personal belongings and temporary housing were covered by their own policies, which avoided angry calls and demands for him to pay out of pocket. The result? Instead of a financial nightmare, the insurance company paid for repairs, the tenants were reimbursed for their losses, and my friend kept collecting rent through his loss of rents rider. The building was fully restored within a year, and his cash flow never collapsed.

Watching him navigate that ordeal was a master class. He didn't get lucky; he got prepared. His coverage decisions were the quiet hero: separate LLC policy, replacement-cost limits, and a strict renter's-insurance clause.

That experience reinforced what I already practice: shop every year, require renter's insurance, and never cut corners on coverage. Insurance is boring—until the day it saves your entire business.

Insurance may not be exciting. You'll never brag about a great premium at a dinner party. But it's the quiet hero of wealth preservation. Real estate builds wealth. Insurance keeps you from losing it overnight. Treat it like a business system: review it, document it, and challenge every renewal. Your portfolio—and your heirs—will thank you.

TAX OPTIMIZATION

Even when I'm not traveling—and I don't travel much—I live a corporate life locally. My immediate team and I often gather for meals where business is front and center. During those lunches or dinners, we discuss management issues, current projects, and future opportunities. These meetings aren't casual get-togethers. They're part of our ongoing corporate culture.

Here's the truth I want you to grasp: business doesn't stop when you leave the office. By blending work with everyday activities—trips, meals, family gatherings—you transform what most people see as personal expenses into legitimate, deductible business functions.

That's not a loophole. That's the way the IRS tax code was written, and the wealthy take advantage of it every single day.

But here's what shocked me when I really started digging in: most people are actually afraid of deductions. For some reason, they feel like they have to pay taxes. They don't want to learn, don't want to question, and almost act brainwashed into believing that taxes are unavoidable and fixed. I've even had family members tell me, "Well, I'd rather just pay my taxes and be done with it." And my reaction is always the same: Who enjoys paying taxes? Certainly not me.

That's why, when I do have downtime, my kids know I'm probably powering through some tax book, studying changes in legislation, and looking for new ways to stay ahead. Out of the eight thousand pages of the IRS tax code, only about four hundred tell you how to pay taxes. The other seventy-six hundred pages are about deductions. Yet the vast majority of people never touch that toolbox. I refuse to live that way. Every deduction I qualify for goes through my tax attorney. I document, document, document—and I sleep easy at night knowing I'm playing by the rules as they were written.

You've all heard people ask, "Why don't the top 1% pay taxes?" Here's why: they understand the rules, and they hire the best tax strategists and attorneys to help them live inside those rules. They know that debt isn't taxed. They know how to leverage deductions. And they use those tools relentlessly.

Take Elon Musk. He doesn't take a big salary. He takes stock, uses it as collateral, and borrows from the bank. The bank is thrilled to loan him money—that's their business. Musk now has millions in cash, completely tax-free. The loan interest is deductible, and when the time comes, he pays it off on his own terms. Totally legal.

It's the same principle I use with my properties. I can refinance, pull equity out tax-free, and redeploy that money into new investments. My company owns my car, pays my insurance, covers my phone, and my PC—because they're business tools. That's not gaming the system. That's following the system as it was designed.

Here's the lesson: stop living like a taxpayer and start living like a strategist. Taxes are one of your largest lifetime expenses, and if you don't learn how to minimize them, you'll never build true generational wealth.

I chose to work with a tax legal firm, and they assisted me with exactly what I needed to properly restructure—not only for tax savings, but also for asset protection and legal structure.

Here's my warning: don't rely on TikTok, Instagram, or random so-called internet gurus for something as serious as your financial future. There's a massive amount of misinformation out there, and if you set things up the wrong way, fixing mistakes later is costly and wasteful. Do it right from the start.

In this chapter, I'll cover some of the key strategies that have helped me reduce my taxes in a major way. Keep in mind: depending on your legal structure—LLC, S-Corp, C-Corp, or Sole Proprietorship—not every strategy will apply equally.

Taxes are emotional for most people. Wealthy investors treat them as mechanical.

The tax code isn't a punishment; it's a rule book. And real estate is one of the most favored asset classes in that rule book.

In addition to using standard tax deductions, I also invest in my properties for the long haul. This is one of the most overlooked but effective strategies for wealthy investors. Rather than writing a check to Uncle Sam, I redirect that money into my buildings. For example, when I put on new siding, replace flooring, or upgrade garage doors, these expenses are deductible. But the beauty is that they don't just save me taxes, they also increase the value of my properties and often reduce expenses or increase revenue.

When I have a big income year, I intentionally accelerate projects. Instead of handing over more money to the IRS, I invest in capital improvements that make my buildings stronger, more efficient, and more profitable. It's a win-win: I protect my income from taxes and create long-term wealth.

In one building, I had a large, underutilized basement. Rather than let it sit empty, I converted it into storage bays. Every dollar I spent on labor and materials was deductible, and at the same time, I created an entirely new revenue stream by renting those storage spaces out to tenants. What was once wasted square footage is now an income-producing asset.

Every time I face a large tax bill, I ask myself, *Would I rather give this to Uncle Sam, or reinvest it into my portfolio?* This is the mindset shift: taxes don't have to be something you fear. You can turn them into a catalyst for growth. The wealthy choose reinvestment. They turn tax liabilities into long-term income streams, higher property values, and stronger portfolios. That's how you scale while keeping more of what you earn.

One year, I had a particularly big income year. I knew Uncle Sam was waiting with both hands out ready to take a huge chunk of it. Instead of writing that check, I looked at one of my properties and saw an opportunity. A fifteen-unit building I owned was running off a single boiler and one hot water tank. The problem? I was paying all the utilities for heat and hot water myself. On average, it was costing me about $12,000 a year. That meant tenants could keep the thermostat up or run hot water all day, and I had no control over the bill. Rather than hand over more money to the government, I reinvested $100,000 into the building to convert it to fifteen separate boilers and hot water systems. Each tenant would now be responsible for their own utilities.

Here's how it played out:

- Because I deducted the full $100,000 as a business expense, I saved $35,000 in taxes immediately (assuming a 35% tax bracket).
- My true out-of-pocket cost was $65,000.
- By eliminating that $12,000 annual utility bill, I improved my Net Operating Income instantly.
- At that rate, the project paid for itself in just over five years.

- Even better, because property values are tied to NOI, my building's appraised value jumped by about $200,000.

Think about that. Instead of writing a check to the IRS, I turned $100,000 into lower expenses, higher cash flow, and a permanent $200,000 boost in equity.

This is the mindset of the wealthy. Taxes aren't just bills; they're signals. Every time I see a big tax bill coming, I ask: *Where can I reinvest this money into my portfolio instead?* And that's how you transform tax liabilities into long-term wealth.

Was it expensive? Yes. But the numbers made sense: I took a large deduction in year one, I cut my operating expenses permanently, and in about six years the project pays for itself—not even counting the tax savings. After that, it's pure profit, and the property's value increased because its operating costs went down.

One of my favorites—especially after the 2025 One Big Beautiful Bill Act (OBBBA) signed by President Trump—is the permanent restoration of 100% bonus depreciation.

BONUS DEPRECIATION: A REAL ESTATE INVESTOR'S SUPERPOWER

What It Is

Bonus depreciation allows investors to immediately expense (write off) certain property components in the year they're placed into service. Normally, buildings depreciate slowly—27.5 years for residential, 39 years for commercial. With the new law, that's changed permanently.

The OBBBA permanently restores 100% bonus depreciation for qualified property acquired and placed in service after January 19, 2025. No more phase-outs. It's full speed ahead.

How It Works (with Cost Segregation)

Not all property ages the same way:

- Appliances, flooring, cabinets = 5–7 years
- Landscaping, parking lots, fencing = 15 years
- Building structure = 27.5 or 39 years

A cost segregation study breaks a property into these buckets. Under OBBBA, you can take 100% of short-lived assets in Year 1.

Why It Matters

- **Massive Year 1 Tax Shield** – Shelter rental income immediately.
- **Supercharged Cash Flow** – Report paper losses while collecting rent.
- **Faster Growth** – Reinvest tax savings into more properties.
- **Certainty** – With 100% expensing permanent, you can plan long-term.

Example: 12-Unit Apartment Acquisition

Purchase Summary

- Purchase Price: $2,100,000
- Market Value: $3,100,000 (instant $1M equity)
- Capital Improvements: $100,000
- Repairs: $120,000

Step 1 – Allocate Land vs. Building

- 20% land = $420,000
- 80% building = $1,680,000 depreciable

Step 2 – Cost Segregation Study

- 5-Year Property: $252,000
- 7-Year Property: $84,000
- 15-Year Property: $168,000
- Remaining Structure: $1,176,000

Step 3 – Apply Bonus Depreciation

- Year 1 deduction = $504,000

Step 4 – Add Repairs & Improvements

- Repairs: $120,000 (deductible immediately)
- Capital Improvements: $3,636 (27.5-year depreciation)
- Regular Building Depreciation: $42,764
- **Total Year 1 Deductions = $670,400**

Step 5 – Tax Impact

- At a 35% federal tax bracket:
- $670,400 × 35% = **$234,640 in tax savings.**

The Big Picture

- Instant equity: +$1M at purchase.
- Property improvements: $220K invested.
- Tax savings: ~$235K in Year 1.

That's like the government funding part of your down payment. Winner, winner—chicken dinner! This is why wealthy investors love real estate. It's not just about rents and appreciation—it's about how the tax code multiplies your growth.

Why I Keep Bonus Depreciation a Bonus

I thought about adjusting my deal analyzer to automatically account for bonus depreciation. On paper, it would make every deal look even more profitable, and frankly, it would push some marginal deals over the line into the buy column. But I made a conscious decision not to do that. Here's why:

3. **Bonus Depreciation Is a Windfall, Not a Guarantee**
    1. Even though the 2025 OBBBA restored 100% bonus depreciation permanently, I still view it as a tax windfall rather than a core underwriting metric. Legislation can change. Tax rules can be rewritten. And not every deal is structured in a way where you'll maximize those deductions. If you base your buy decision on a tax benefit and then it disappears, the deal itself might not stand on its own.
    2. **Conservative Underwriting Protects You**
    3. My philosophy is simple: the deal has to work on its own fundamentals—cash flow, equity, and market strength. If the property can pay for itself and hit my return goals without bonus depreciation, then when I *do* apply it, it's just extra. That's how I sleep at night knowing I didn't stretch for a deal that only penciled out because of a tax perk.
    4. **Bonus Depreciation Is "Icing on the Cake"**
    5. When you get it, it's phenomenal—tens or even hundreds of thousands in upfront tax savings. But it shouldn't be the cake itself. Think of it as your surprise gift: it accelerates your growth, pays down debt faster, or fuels your next acquisition. But it's not something I want to rely on when deciding if a deal is good or not.
    6. **Protecting Others**
    7. I don't just think about my portfolio. I think about my partners, investors, and even family members who may eventually inherit my properties. If I built my underwriting models around bonus depreciation, I'd be tempting others to take risks they might not fully understand. Leaving it out ensures everyone approaches deals with a margin of safety.

The Bottom Line

When I run my numbers, I want the deal to make sense without bonus depreciation. If the fundamentals check out, then I know I'm buying a strong, safe asset. When bonus depreciation gets applied on top, that's just free acceleration—an extra lever to grow wealth faster. It's like getting the keys to a Ferrari when you already owned a reliable truck. Nice to have, but not something you rely on to get from point A to point B.

After cost segregation, my next most powerful tax deduction comes from what I call "living corporate life."

How to Turn a Tax Bill Into an Asset

1. **Spot the Tax Bill Coming**

Review your income during the year. If you're staring at a big tax bill, ask: *Can I reinvest this instead of sending it to the IRS?*

2. **Identify High-Impact Projects**

Look for upgrades that reduce expenses (e.g., converting utilities, installing energy-efficient systems) or increase revenue (e.g., adding storage units, upgrading finishes to justify higher rents).

3. **Run the Numbers**

Calculate the tax savings (investment × tax rate). Subtract that from the project cost to find your true after-tax outlay. Estimate annual savings or new income created. Divide to find your payback period.

4. **Measure the Value Boost**

Divide your annual NOI improvement by the cap rate. This tells you how much value the project added to your property.

Example: $12,000 savings ÷ 6% = $200,000 increase in property value.

5. **Execute and Document**

Complete the project before year-end to lock in deductions. Keep invoices, contracts, and proof of payment.

6. **Reap the Benefits**

Pay less tax today. Enjoy reduced expenses or new income streams tomorrow. Build long-term equity and wealth automatically.

REINVESTING IN PROPERTIES AS A TAX STRATEGY

Most investors treat taxes as an unavoidable expense. I learned to treat them as a signal. A growing tax bill usually means one thing: income is increasing. That's not a problem—it's feedback. The question is how you respond to it.

Early on, my instinct was the same as most people's: minimize the damage. Pay the bill. Move on. Eventually, I realized that the reaction was backwards. Instead of asking, *How do I reduce this?* I started asking a better question: How do I convert this obligation into another income-producing asset?

Reinvestment became the answer. Rather than pulling money out of the system, I pushed it back in—upgrading properties, increasing NOI, and strengthening the long-term performance of assets I already owned.

Reinvestment does several things simultaneously:

- Reduces taxable income
- Improves tenant experience
- Raises rents legitimately
- Increases property value
- Improves future refinancing outcomes

This is not theoretical. Small, intentional upgrades done at the right time can permanently change a building's trajectory.

One of the most vivid examples in my career came when I bought an eighteen-unit building with a daycare center from the bank. It was a foreclosure, and to say it was a mess would be an understatement. The previous landlord—a textbook slumlord—had run it straight into the ground. He collected rent, ignored repairs, and deferred every ounce of maintenance until the property collapsed financially.

When I first walked the property, it was clear this wasn't going to be a paint-and-carpet project. It was a gut job. The hallways smelled of neglect, the systems were outdated or broken, and tenants had grown used to living in subpar conditions. The daycare center, which should have been a community asset, was run down and almost unusable. Most investors would have walked away. But I saw an opportunity. Because it was bank-owned, I was able to buy the building for $500,000. Instead of patching it up like the previous owner, I went all-in. I invested $800,000 into new systems, fresh renovations, and structural upgrades to make the property not just livable but desirable. I didn't cut corners. I rebuilt it to last.

The transformation was dramatic. Tenants who had been on the verge of leaving were suddenly proud to live there. I cleaned up the daycare center so it could be reactivated, which not only generated rent but also served as a benefit to the families in the building and neighborhood. Occupancy stabilized, cash flow improved, and the property's reputation turned around.

And here's the payoff: after all the work, I sold the building for $3.1 million.

The profit from that sale was only part of the story. Along the way, the $800,000 renovation wasn't just money out the door; it was a massive tax shield. With cost segregation and bonus depreciation, I was able to write off large portions of those improvements in the very first year. That meant I wasn't just building equity, I was also slashing my taxable income.

Think about it:

- All-in Investment: $1.3 million ($500k purchase + $800k renovations)
- Sale Price: $3.1 million
- Equity Gain: $1.8 million, plus improved cash flow while I owned it.
- Tax Benefit: Hundreds of thousands in upfront deductions through depreciation, which helped offset income from my other properties.

This is the beauty of real estate. The IRS code is written in a way that rewards investors who improve housing and build community. A slumlord would have left this building to rot. I turned it into a long-term asset, created wealth, and legally reduced my taxes while doing it.

It was a good property, but I ended up selling it, not because I wanted to. The decision came down to the fact that I was in a partnership at the time, and my partner wanted to sell. If it had been solely up to me, I never would have let it go. My philosophy has always been clear: I don't sell. My strategy is to hold onto great assets indefinitely, refinance them when needed, and use that capital to keep buying more properties.

Hold onto great assets indefinitely, refinance them when needed, and use that capital to keep buying more properties.

Selling might give you a one-time payday, but holding gives you generational wealth. A property that's producing cash flow, appreciating in value, and offering tax advantages is far too valuable to walk away from. For me, real estate isn't about quick flips—it's about building a machine that can sustain my family, and eventually my kids and grandkids, for decades.

Why I Don't Sell

- Cash Flow Never Stops—Selling gives you a one-time payday. Holding gives you a monthly cash flow for life.
- Appreciation Builds Equity—Over time, properties increase in value. Selling cuts off future appreciation.
- Tax Advantages Multiply—Depreciation, cost segregation, and bonus depreciation offset income year after year. Selling triggers capital gains and recapture taxes unless you use a 1031 exchange as a strategy.
- Refinancing Unlocks Capital—Instead of selling, I refinance. That gives me tax-free cash I can use to buy more assets—while keeping the property.
- Generational Wealth—The real goal isn't a quick flip. It's handing my kids and grandkids a portfolio of strong, cash-flowing properties that will last for decades.

My wife and I go back and forth on this all the time. She'll say, "Let's sell a few of the smaller buildings and use the money to buy something bigger." But my philosophy is different. Why sell when you don't have to?

Instead, I'd rather refinance the property, pull out tax-free capital, and use that money to buy the next building. Sometimes I'll refinance two smaller properties together to move into a much larger asset, all while holding on to the originals. That way, the portfolio keeps growing without shrinking.

Now, yes—I could sell and avoid taxes by doing a 1031 exchange. And for many investors, that's a fantastic strategy. But for me, the true key to building generational wealth is holding the asset. The refinance model lets me keep the building, keep the cash flow, and still expand the portfolio without handing a dime to Uncle Sam.

And since I brought up the 1031 exchange, some of you are probably wondering: *What exactly is a 1031 exchange?* Let me explain…

WHAT IS A 1031 EXCHANGE?

A 1031 exchange—named after Section 1031 of the IRS tax code—is one of the most powerful tools available to real estate investors. In simple terms, it allows you to defer paying capital gains taxes when you sell an investment property, as long as you reinvest the proceeds into another property of equal or greater value. Instead of writing a massive check to Uncle Sam after a sale, you keep that money working for you in your next deal.

Think of it like buying houses in Monopoly. You sell one green property, but instead of paying taxes on your profit, you roll all your winnings directly into the next hotel upgrade. The game continues, and your capital keeps growing.

How It Works

1. Sell Your Investment Property
2. You sell a property you've held for investment purposes (not your primary residence).
3. Hire a Qualified Intermediary (QI)
4. The proceeds go to a third-party intermediary; you can't touch the cash yourself.
5. Identify Replacement Property
6. Within 45 days, you must formally identify potential replacement properties.
7. Close on Replacement
8. Within 180 days, you must purchase the replacement property (or properties) using the exchange funds.

If you follow the rules, the IRS lets you defer all capital gains taxes, including depreciation recapture.

The Positives

- Tax Deferral Superpower
- Instead of giving 20–30% of your gain to the IRS, you keep it all invested in real estate. This accelerates portfolio growth.
- Leverage Growth
- By rolling equity forward, you can trade up from a small property into larger, more profitable assets—without losing capital to taxes.
- Generational Planning
- If you continue doing 1031 exchanges throughout your lifetime and pass the properties to your heirs, they receive a step-up in basis. That means all those deferred taxes vanish at death. Your kids inherit the property tax-free at market value.

The Negatives

- Strict Deadlines
- The 45-day identification and 180-day closing rules are rigid. Miss them, and the exchange is disqualified.
- Like-Kind Requirement
- You can't swap an apartment building for stocks or gold. It has to be like-kind real estate (though the IRS defines this broadly, meaning almost any investment real estate can qualify).
- Reduced Flexibility
- Because your funds are locked with a qualified intermediary, you lose flexibility. You may feel pressure to buy a property quickly, even if it's not the best deal, just to avoid triggering taxes.
- Kicks the Can Down the Road
- A 1031 doesn't eliminate taxes; it defers them. Unless you hold the property until death and pass it to heirs, you'll eventually face a tax bill when you cash out.

The Bottom Line

A 1031 exchange is one of the most powerful wealth-building tools in the tax code. It allows you to compound real estate gains tax-deferred, trading up from smaller properties to bigger, more profitable ones. But it comes with strict rules and requires careful planning. Used strategically, it can be a cornerstone of generational wealth building—but it's not something to jump into without guidance from a tax strategist or attorney who specializes in exchanges.

Let's say you bought a small six-unit building years ago for $700,000. Over time, it appreciated, and now you're selling it for $1.2 million.

- **Original Purchase Price:** $700,000
- **Sale Price:** $1,200,000
- **Gain:** $500,000

If you sell outright without a 1031 exchange, Uncle Sam steps in:

- Federal capital gains tax (20%): $100,000
- Depreciation recapture (25% on what you wrote off over the years, let's say $50,000): $50,000
- State taxes (varies, but let's assume 5%): $25,000

That's a total tax bill of about $175,000. Instead of reinvesting $500,000 of profit, you'd only have about $325,000 left after taxes.

Now let's look at the same sale using a 1031 exchange:

- You roll the full $500,000 gain into a new property.
- You identify a twelve-unit building priced at $2 million.
- You use your $500,000 as the down payment and finance the rest.

Result: instead of shrinking your buying power with taxes, you leveraged the full $500,000 to scale into a bigger property with more units, more income, and more long-term appreciation potential.

The 1031 exchange keeps your capital working for you. It's like playing real estate with the IRS's money. You defer taxes, buy bigger properties, and accelerate your portfolio growth. If you keep doing this, trading up over and over and then passing the properties to your kids, the deferred taxes disappear thanks to the step-up in basis.

This is where the step-up in basis becomes one of the most powerful—and least understood—wealth tools in the tax code. Step-up in basis means that when you pass away, the tax basis of your real estate is reset to its current fair market value, not what you originally paid for it. All of the appreciation that occurred during your lifetime—and all the depreciation you took along the way—essentially disappears for tax purposes. Your heirs start fresh, as if they bought the property on the day they inherited it.

Here's a simple example. Let's say you bought a small apartment building years ago for $500,000. Over time, you depreciated the property and refinanced it, pulling out equity tax-free to buy more assets. Fast-forward twenty-five years, and that same building is now worth $1.5 million. If you sold it while alive, you'd face capital gains taxes, depreciation recapture, and possibly state taxes—easily hundreds of thousands of dollars.

But if you hold that property and pass it to your children, the IRS "steps up" the basis to $1.5 million. If your kids sell it the next day for $1.5 million, they owe zero capital gains tax. If they hold it, they begin depreciating the property again based on the new, higher value. It's as if the tax clock was reset.

That's why long-term real estate investors focus on deferral, not avoidance. You defer taxes through depreciation and 1031 exchanges, grow your portfolio using leverage and refinancing, and then let the step-up in basis eliminate the deferred taxes entirely at death. It's legal, it's intentional, and it's exactly how generational wealth is built.

This is the endgame. You're not just trading up into bigger properties; you're creating a tax-efficient bridge that allows wealth to move from one generation to the next without being shredded by the IRS. Your kids don't inherit your tax problems. They inherit clean assets, fresh depreciation, and a portfolio positioned to keep growing.

That's not an accident. That's strategy. That's why savvy investors call the 1031 "the ultimate compounding machine" in real estate.

I know many investors who have used them successfully, and I've even advised others through the process. But for me, given my generational wealth strategy, I haven't felt the need to take that path yet. My approach has always been focused on refinancing and holding. That said, I absolutely see a day in the future when I may use a 1031 exchange if it aligns with the bigger picture. It's a powerful tool.

A few years back, I owned a mid-size apartment building that had appreciated significantly since I bought it. At the time, I had two options: I could sell it, pocket the profit, and pay capital gains and depreciation recapture taxes. Or I could refinance it.

I chose the refinance route.

Here's how it worked:

- **Original Purchase Price:** $1.2 million
- **Loan Paid Down to** $800,000
- **New Appraisal:** $2.5 million
- **Refinance Loan (70% LTV):** $1.75 million

That refinance gave me about $950,000 in cash at closing ($1.75M new loan – $800k old loan), and here's the kicker: it was completely tax-free. Instead of writing a massive check to Uncle Sam, I took that $950,000 and used it as the down payment on my next property. I kept the original building, which continued to cash flow, and I added another asset to my portfolio that began generating income and appreciating in value.

When you sell, you hand a big portion of your profit over to the IRS. When you refinance, you get the same access to capital but tax-free—and you keep the property working for you. This is how the wealthy grow portfolios without draining equity or shrinking their balance sheet.

That's why my rule is simple: don't sell, refinance.

THE WEALTH CYCLE

1. **Buy Smart**

- Purchase under market value or distressed properties.
- Look for hidden opportunities: foreclosures, value-add potential, deferred maintenance.

2. **Improve the Asset**

- Renovate, upgrade systems, add amenities, and raise rents.
- Every dollar added to NOI increases property value.

3. **Refinance, Don't Sell**

- Reappraise the improved property.
- Pull out tax-free cash through refinancing.
- Keep the property generating cash flow and appreciation.

4. **Buy More**

- Use refinance proceeds as down payments on new acquisitions.
- Scale your portfolio without selling or paying capital gains.

5. **Repeat the Cycle**

- Each round compounds your equity, cash flow, and net worth.

- Over time, your portfolio becomes a self-funding wealth machine.

Selling is a one-time event. Refinancing lets you multiply assets, defer taxes, and build generational wealth without breaking the cycle.

THE WEALTHY MINDSET

For me, every improvement is about more than just a short-term return. When I replace systems, upgrade units, or renovate common areas, I don't look for the cheapest shortcut. I am not a slumlord by any stretch of the imagination. That's not who I am, and it's not the legacy I want to leave behind. I invest in my buildings, I take pride in maintaining them, and I constantly look for ways to create more income while also increasing value. I do it right the first time because I know that work will outlast me.

That long-term vision is what drives me. I don't just own properties for today's cash flow—I own them for the next generation. My kids will one day inherit this portfolio, and when they do, I want them to step into well-maintained, upgraded buildings that will last another twenty, thirty, or even forty years without major headaches.

I've seen too many landlords kick the can down the road, patching roofs instead of replacing them, ignoring leaks instead of fixing them. That may save money today, but it creates a bigger, more expensive problem tomorrow. I'd rather invest now, knowing that when my kids take over, they won't inherit deferred maintenance. They'll inherit strong, cash-flowing assets that are built to last.

This is the difference between a shortsighted landlord and a true investor. A slumlord bleeds a property dry, cutting corners and collecting every dollar they can today without a care for tomorrow. A real investor thinks like a builder, not just an owner. I ask myself: *What can I do today that will make this property stronger, more valuable, and easier to manage for the next twenty years?*

That mindset pays off two ways:

1. My tenants enjoy safe, clean, well-maintained homes—which means fewer vacancies and higher retention.
2. My kids will inherit a machine that runs, not a mess they have to fix.

. . .

That's the true power of real estate done right. It's not just about maximizing today's returns; it's about leaving behind an asset that lasts for generations.

SLUMLORD VS. INVESTOR MINDSET

Slumlord Mentality	True Investor Mentality
Cuts corners on repairs.	Fixes problems at the root that extend building life.
Squeezes every dollar today with no thought for tomorrow.	Thinks generationally, building equity, stability, and longevity for family and tenants.
Views tenants as a burden and expense.	Views tenants as customers, providing quality homes increases retention and income.
Defers maintenance until it becomes an emergency.	Proactively renovates and upgrades, reducing future costs and preserving value.
Leaves kids or heirs with headaches, lawsuits, and rundown properties.	Leaves kids with a well-oiled machine that makes an income and appreciates in value.
Reputation: bottom-feeder landlord	Reputation: respected investor, community builder, and legacy planner.

Slumlords play for pennies today; investors play for dollars tomorrow. I've chosen to be the latter. Every decision I make is not just about my own cash flow. It's about the quality of life for my tenants and the generational wealth and security I'm leaving to my kids.

Structure, insurance, and tax strategy don't remove risk. They make risk manageable. Every layer serves a purpose:

- LLCs isolate
- Insurance absorbs

- Taxes redirect

Together, they create durability.

Durability is what separates investors who survive decades from those who flame out after a few wins. At this stage, your portfolio is no longer fragile. It's protected, insured, and optimized. But protection alone doesn't create momentum.

In the next chapter, we move into advanced execution—how to maximize deductions, take advantage of tax shelters, value adds to your properties, refinance strategically, and multiply income without simply buying more properties.

CHAPTER 7
ADVANCED REAL ESTATE STRATEGIES

I've built my life and my family's life around the idea that we aren't just individuals, we are a company. That means I've surrounded myself with a team: my wife, my three kids, extended family members, and even trusted advisors who together form the board of advisors for my management company.

This isn't just symbolic; it's structured. Each person has a role, responsibilities, and input into how the company (and the family portfolio) grows. Because of that, many of the activities we take part in together are legitimate, deductible business functions.

For example, I no longer think of vacations in the traditional sense. Instead, I blend travel with business by holding an annual board retreat. We may pick a destination, but it's not just about relaxation; it's about strategy. I create a detailed itinerary and daily agenda where we review:

- Management performance of our properties.
- Financials, cash flow, and capital improvements.
- Growth strategies, acquisitions, and financing opportunities.
- Long-term planning for generational wealth and family involvement.

By documenting agendas, meeting minutes, and outcomes, these trips qualify as business retreats. The result? I get the best of both worlds: quality time with my family and advisors in a beautiful location, while also making the costs legally deductible business expenses.

The key lesson here is this: wealthy investors don't separate their personal and professional lives in rigid boxes. They align them. They live in such a way that family, lifestyle, and business are interconnected, producing not only stronger relationships and better decision-making but also powerful tax advantages. Wealthy investors don't just invest in properties; they build a corporate ecosystem around themselves.

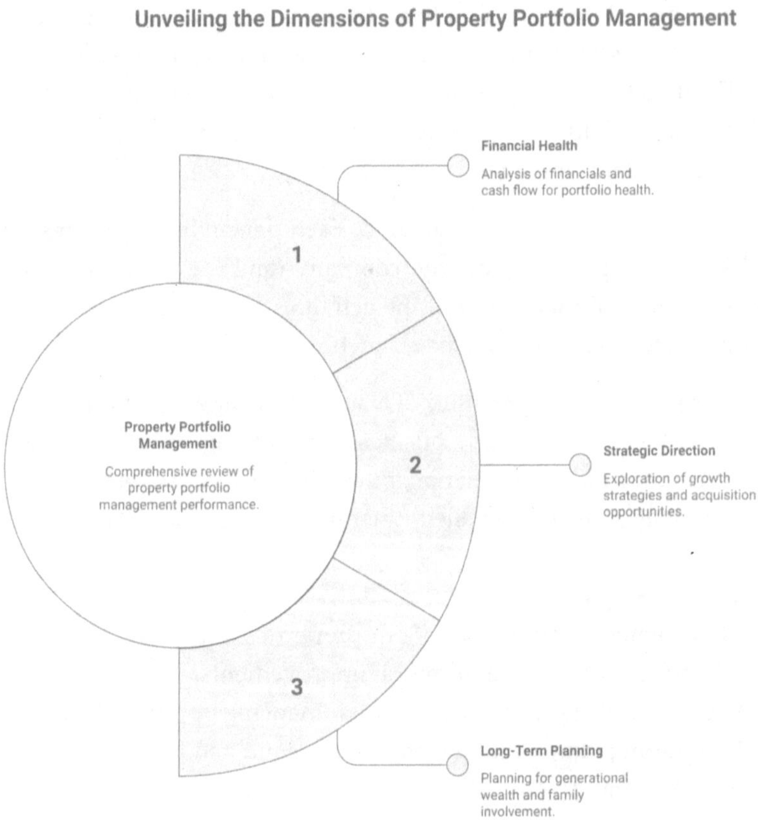

ALIGNING FAMILY AND BUSINESS:

Create a Family Board of Advisors

- Appoint members from your spouse, kids, extended family, and trusted colleagues.
- Assign each person a defined role (finance, operations, acquisitions, tenant relations, marketing, etc.).
- Formalize it with board charters or role descriptions.

Why? It creates accountability, trains the next generation, and builds legitimacy for family involvement.

Hold Structured Meetings

- Schedule quarterly meetings (virtual or in person).
- Keep agendas with topics like property updates, financial performance, and future goals.
- Take minutes documenting attendance, discussions, and decisions.

Why? Written records show the IRS that these are legitimate business meetings.

Annual Board Retreats

- Pick a destination but treat it as business first, leisure second.
- Prepare a detailed itinerary: each day includes a business session, such as Property Management and Maintenance Review, Expansion/Acquisition Strategies, Tax and Legal Updates, Succession and Generational Planning.
- Document attendance, topics, and action steps.

Why? This transforms what could be considered a vacation into a deductible business retreat.

Blend Family and Business Roles

- Kids can be given age-appropriate roles: helping with marketing, bookkeeping, or tenant communications.
- Spouses may handle administration, finance, or HR.
- Extended family or professionals can serve as advisors on legal, tax, or lending matters.

Why? This creates alignment—your family isn't just inheriting wealth, they're learning to manage and grow it.

Document Everything

- Keep itineraries, agendas, minutes, receipts, and photos of meetings.
- Use accounting software (QuickBooks, etc.) to categorize expenses clearly.
- Maintain a Board Binder (physical or digital) for IRS audit protection.

Why? Proper documentation is the difference between a legitimate deduction and a denied one.

Reap the Benefits

- Deductible travel, lodging, and meals related to board activities.
- Stronger family unity through shared purpose.
- Training the next generation to think like owners, not employees.
- A lifestyle where family, fun, and business reinforce each other instead of competing.

Outside of my annual board retreat, I also take other trips throughout the year that legitimately qualify as business-related. For example, I travel to Arizona once a year to meet with my tax attorney. Not only do I schedule this in the winter so I can escape the cold in New Jersey, but I also maximize the trip by reviewing strategies, updating my tax planning, and setting goals for the year.

I also have extended family in California and Seattle who are active in real estate. When I visit them, those trips aren't just personal—they're working trips. We exchange ideas, compare market conditions, and discuss best practices in acquisitions, management, and financing. Because the business component is real and documented, these trips qualify as deductible expenses.

Even when I'm not on the road—and truthfully, I don't travel much—I live and breathe corporate life right here at home. My team and I often gather for lunches or dinners where business is always at the forefront. These aren't casual get-togethers. They're intentional meetings where we talk through management issues, current projects, and future opportunities. It's our way of building and reinforcing the culture of our company.

What you start to realize is this: business doesn't stop when you walk out of the office. When you adopt a corporate mindset, everyday life becomes an extension of business. Meals, trips, and even family gatherings can become legitimate, deductible business functions when they are tied directly to the growth and operation of the company. These aren't loopholes; they're written into the tax code and used by the wealthy every single day.

The reality is that only a small percentage of people ever figure this out. Most people stay stuck in the cycle of a traditional job, which I call the worst money you can earn. W-2 income is taxed heavily, offers few deductions, and rarely builds true financial security. But once you layer in a business—even a side business—you unlock an entirely new set of tools: deductions, credits, protections, and the framework to build generational wealth.

Once you structure your life like a company, tax efficiency becomes part of your lifestyle

This is where trusts come into play. I use both irrevocable and revocable trusts to protect assets, shield my family's wealth, and create structure for the next generation. Later in this book, I'll also show you how life insurance becomes a cornerstone of that system, serving as both protection and growth.

When you finally begin to leverage the eight thousand pages of the U.S. tax code, you understand what I discovered: my company owns my phone, my computer, my car, and even pays for my car insurance. These aren't luxuries. They're strategic, legal advantages that shift the game in your favor. Once you adopt this structure, you stop playing defense with money and start playing offense.

This ties back to your theme: once you structure your life like a company, tax efficiency becomes part of your lifestyle, not just a once-a-year filing event.

ADVANCED TAX STRATEGIES FOR LLC OWNERS

The Home Office Deduction

If you're running your business from home, don't skip the home office deduction. Too many people take the simplified method—just a flat $1,500 per year—but that leaves money on the table. Instead, I recommend the regular method, which lets you deduct the actual business-use percentage of your home. Here's how it works:

- Calculate the square footage of your home office divided by the total square footage of your house.
- Apply that percentage to household expenses like utilities, internet, insurance, and even a portion of your mortgage interest or rent.

For example, if your home office is 10% of your house, then 10% of your electric bill, property taxes, and internet can be written off as a business expense. It takes a little more tracking, but the savings are real. When I first did this, I couldn't believe the difference—it was thousands of dollars that would have otherwise gone untapped.

Equipment and Cell Phones

When I buy a new phone, laptop, printer, or even basic office supplies like paper and ink, those aren't personal expenses. They're legitimate business deductions. The key is keeping clean records. Every time I upgrade my phone, I run it through the business because I use it daily for tenants, contractors, lenders, and partners. The same goes for laptops. I don't buy them as luxuries; I buy them because they're tools of the trade.

One important note: you should maintain a separate home or personal phone line to clearly demonstrate to the IRS that there's a distinction between business and personal use. That separation helps protect the deduction and avoids any questions if you're ever audited.

Vehicle Deductions – Code Section 179 & Section 168(k)

Vehicles can be a gold mine for deductions if structured correctly. The rule of thumb: the vehicle must be used for business more than 50% of the time. Keep a mileage log, record business trips, and be diligent.

Here's the kicker: under Section 179 and Section 168(k), you can deduct the full purchase price of certain heavy vehicles (over six thousand pounds gross vehicle weight rating). A few years ago, before bonus depreciation was restored, I bought a qualifying SUV under my business. Because it was over the six-thousand-pound threshold, I was able to write off the entire purchase in the first year. That's like the IRS paying part of your down payment for your car.

The Augusta Rule

This one feels almost too good to be true—but it's right in the tax code. The Augusta Rule allows you to rent out your personal residence to your business for up to fourteen days per year, tax-free. The company gets to deduct the expense, and you don't have to report the rental income.

Personally, I don't use all fourteen days. I think that's aggressive. Instead, I plan about a week per year where I host meetings, strategy sessions, and presentations at my home. To stay compliant, I pull comps by finding VRBO or Airbnb rentals in my area that are similar to my house, save that data in my files, and keep a detailed agenda with meeting minutes.

The key to making this work: document, document, document.

Marketing and Advertising

Every postcard mailed, every Facebook ad run, every website built—it's all tax-deductible. I see marketing as an investment, not an expense. Every dollar I put into reaching tenants or finding deals gets written off against my income. It's one of the simplest, most straight-forward deductions, and yet many small landlords underutilize it.

Real Estate Professional Status - One of the Best Job Combinations for Married Couples

This is the holy grail of tax planning for serious investors. It's not about how many units you own—it's about your time commitment. If you or your spouse qualify, your rental real estate activity is treated as an active business. That means all those powerful depreciation deductions (including bonus depreciation) can be used to offset W-2 or 1099 income.

I've seen families save tens of thousands—sometimes hundreds of thousands—by strategically designating the spouse who's most involved as the real estate professional. It's a game-changer.

One of the most powerful wealth-building job combinations early on for married couples is when one spouse is a high W-2 income earner, and the other qualifies as a Real Estate Professional.

This is exactly what my wife and I did — and it is a strategy I have recommended to countless others over the years because of how effective it can be when executed properly.

A Real Estate Professional is a special designation defined by the IRS. This status allows married couples to dramatically reduce — and in many cases legally eliminate — federal income taxes when combined with the tax strategies outlined throughout this book.

This is not a loophole.

It is an explicit designation written directly into the tax code.

What Is a Real Estate Professional?

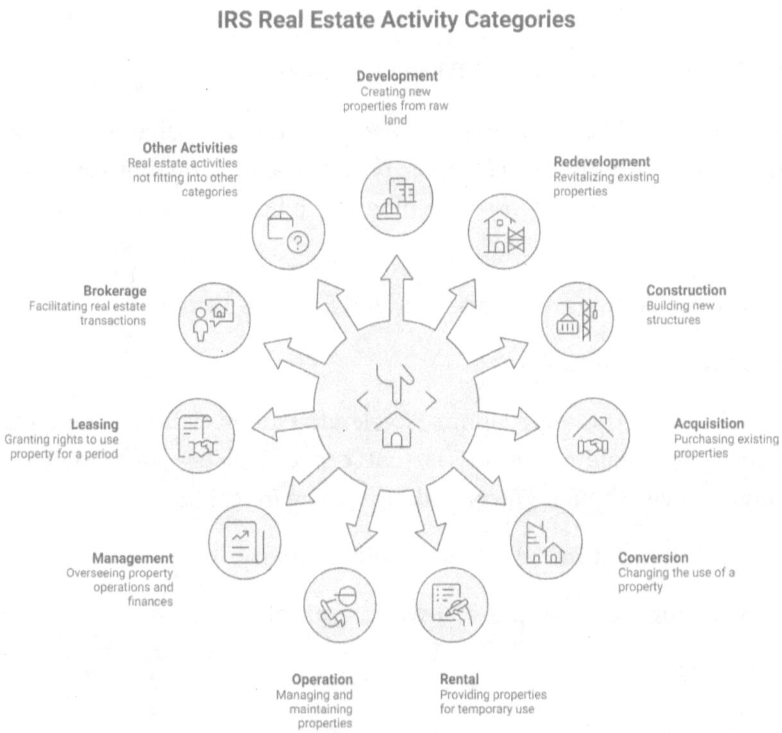

To qualify, you must materially participate in one or more of these categories.

On your tax return, there is literally a checkbox that asks:

"Are you a real estate professional?"

But to legally check that box, two requirements must be met:

1. You must work at least 750 hours per year in qualifying real estate activities
2. Real estate must be your primary occupation (more than any other job)

For married couples, here is the key advantage:

Only one spouse needs to qualify — but the tax benefits apply to both.

This is where the strategy becomes a home run.

Why This Is So Powerful for Married Couples

Normally, rental real estate losses are considered passive losses and cannot offset W-2 income. However, once one spouse qualifies as a *Real Estate Professional*, rental losses become active losses, which means they can be used to offset:

W-2 income, Bonuses, Commissions, and Business income

This unlocks the ability to use:

Depreciation, Cost segregation, Accelerated depreciation, Operating expenses to create paper losses that can completely offset taxable income — even though you're making money in real life.

Example: Buying a $600,000 Four-Family Property

Let's walk through a simple, real-world example.

Purchase Details

Purchase price: $600,000

Land value (non-depreciable): $100,000

Building value: $500,000

Loan: 80% financed

Property is a long-term rental

Cost Segregation Study

A typical cost segregation study on a small multifamily property may accelerate approximately 25–30% of the building value.

Let's assume 30% for this example.

Accelerated depreciation:

$500,000 × 30% = $150,000

Under current tax rules, much of this can be depreciated in the first year.

Annual Operating Numbers

Rental income: $72,000

Expenses (repairs, insurance, taxes, management, utilities, mileage, etc.): $32,000

Net operating income before depreciation: $40,000

Apply Depreciation

Cost segregation depreciation: $150,000

Regular depreciation (remaining portion): included but ignored here for simplicity

Final Tax Result (Paper Loss)

Item	Amount
Net operating income	+$40,000
Accelerated depreciation	−$150,000
Total paper loss	*−$110,000*

Even though the property *cash flows positively*, the IRS sees:

A $110,000 loss

Offset W-2 Income

Now, assume the other spouse earns:

- W-2 income: $180,000

Because one spouse qualifies as a *Real Estate Professional*, the $110,000 loss can legally offset W-2 income:

Income	Amount
W-2 income	$180,000
Real estate loss	−$110,000
Taxable income	$70,000

That means the couple just eliminated tax on $110,000 of income — legally.

At a combined federal and state marginal rate of ~35%, that's roughly:

$38,500 in taxes saved — in year one.

And remember:

- You still own the property
- You still have appreciation
- You still have a loan paydown
- You still have cash flow

This is how wealthy families legally compound faster.

Why This Strategy Changes Everything

When you combine:

- A high W-2 income
- A Real Estate Professional spouse
- Rental property ownership
- Cost segregation
- Proper bookkeeping
- Strategic tax planning

You create a system where:

- Income is earned
- Taxes are minimized
- Wealth compounds faster
- Capital can be reinvested

This is not aggressive.

This is not risky.

This is simply understanding the rules that already exist.

The wealthy don't avoid taxes —

they understand the tax code better than everyone else.

Family Payroll

One of the most overlooked tax strategies for business owners is hiring your own children. The IRS allows you to pay your kids a reasonable wage for legitimate work in your business, and if you do it correctly, it can save thousands in taxes every year while teaching them financial literacy.

Over Eighteen

My kids are now over eighteen. I put them to work in the business and issue them 1099s for the services they provide. Each earns $9,800 per year. Out of that, I have them contribute the maximum allowed—$7,000 per year—into a Roth IRA. This accomplishes two things:

1. I get the deduction for paying them.
2. They get an automatic savings and investment plan that grows tax-free for life.

We already walked through the math, but here it is again because it's powerful:

- $7,000/year from age eighteen to fifty = $224,000 invested.
- At 9% average growth, that becomes $1,148,259 by age fifty.
- Nearly $925,000 of that is growth, and all of it is tax-free.

Under Eighteen

Every family member can play a role in the business, and the tax code rewards you for it. When my kids were minors, I still was able to pay them for work they performed.

Why It Works

- **Deductible Expense for You:** Wages you pay your child are a business expense, reducing your taxable income.

- **Tax-Free Income for Them:** As of 2025, a child can earn up to $13,850 (the standard deduction) without paying federal income tax. That means the first $13,850 you pay them is essentially tax-free income.
- **No Payroll Taxes in Certain Cases:** If your business is an LLC (taxed as a sole proprietorship) or a partnership owned only by you and your spouse, wages paid to your kids under eighteen are not subject to Social Security or Medicare taxes. (If you're taxed as an S-Corp or C-Corp, payroll taxes apply, but the strategy can still be worthwhile.)

What They Can Do

The key is that your kids must actually perform real work appropriate for their age. Examples include:

- Filing, shredding, and organizing documents.
- Cleaning and maintaining rental properties.
- Helping with social media, photography, and marketing.
- Bookkeeping support, scanning receipts, data entry.
- Yard work or property upkeep.

This isn't about "free money." It's about involving your kids in the family business and teaching them the value of work and responsibility.

How Much You Can Deduct

You can pay them up to the standard deduction amount ($13,850 in 2025) tax-free. Anything above that would be taxed at their rate, which is still typically much lower than yours. For example:

- You pay your fifteen-year-old $10,000 for a year of work.
- You deduct $10,000 as a business expense.

- Your child owes zero federal income tax since it's under the $13,850 standard deduction.
- No payroll taxes apply if structured under an LLC/sole prop.

That's a direct tax savings to your business while shifting income into your child's hands tax-free. Here's where it gets powerful: once your child has earned income, they can contribute to a Roth IRA. Imagine paying your fifteen-year-old $10,000, then having them contribute $7,000 into a Roth IRA each year. That money grows tax-free for decades, turning small teenage paychecks into hundreds of thousands of dollars by the time they retire.

This is exactly how you transform a deduction today into generational wealth tomorrow.

How to Operate Legally

If you treat your business like a real job, the IRS will too. When you are hiring family members, you have to be professional.

- Keep detailed job descriptions and document their work.
- Pay by check or direct deposit into an account in their name.
- Track hours worked and maintain a simple timesheet.
- Issue a W-2 at year-end if your business structure requires it.
- Make sure the pay is reasonable for the work performed.

The Bottom Line

Hiring your kids under eighteen is one of the cleanest, most powerful tax strategies available to small business owners. You lower your own taxable income, your kids earn tax-free wages, and together you build a foundation of work ethic, financial literacy, and long-term wealth.

Tax Hacks Quick Reference for Real Estate Investors

Strategy	How It Works	Key Benefit	Pro Tip
Home Office Deduction	Deduct business-use % of your home (utilities, internet, insurance, mortgage).	Saves thousands beyond simplified $1,500 limit.	Use the regular method (square footage) and keep utility/tax receipts.
Equipment & Phones	Deduct laptops, phones, printers, ink, paper, and other office gear.	Everyday items become business write-offs.	Always buy through the business and log usage.
Vehicle Deduction	Deduct mileage or actual costs if >50% business use. Section 179 allows full expensing of vehicles >6,000 lbs.	Large upfront write-offs.	Buy heavy vehicles in business name; track mileage with an app.
Augusta Rule	Rent your house to your LLC/corp up to 14 days per year tax-free.	Dual benefit: corp deducts, you pay no tax.	Document comps (Airbnb/VRBO), agendas, and meeting minutes.
Marketing & Advertising	Deduct all advertising expenses (flyers, signs, online ads, websites).	Turns marketing into a full write-off.	Track ROI by property or campaign.
Real Estate Professional Status	Qualify by 750+ hours AND 50%+ of time in real estate activities.	Allows depreciation to offset W-2/1099 income.	Often spouse can qualify—plan strategically.
Hire Kids Under 18	Pay kids a reasonable wage for real work in your business. Wages deductible to you, tax-free to them up to $13,850/year.	Shifts income into a zero-tax bracket, builds work ethic.	Document job duties, track hours, pay by check. Bonus: open a Roth IRA with their earnings.
1099 Family Members (18+)	Pay kids/spouse reasonable wages for work done. Kids can fund Roth IRAs.	Income shifts to lower brackets + builds wealth.	Issue 1099s, pay up to $9,800, direct $7,000 into Roth IRAs.
Roth IRA Compounding	Tax-free retirement growth from consistent contributions.	Turns $224k into $1.15M tax-free by age 50.	Start kids at 18, automate contributions, let compounding work.
Tax hacks like these aren't loopholes—they're strategies written into the code. Wealthy investors don't ignore them; they design their lives around them.			

Utilizing Independent Retirement Accounts (IRAs)One of the smartest strategies is leveraging retirement accounts, specifically a self-directed IRA (SDIRA). Unlike a traditional IRA that limits you to stocks and mutual funds, with a self-directed IRA you can invest in real estate, notes, private lending, or even syndications. That means I can align my retirement investments with what I already know and excel at—real estate. And investing in an IRA allows you to take money that would otherwise go straight to Uncle Sam in taxes and redirect it into an account that can legally grow tax-deferred or even tax-free.

TRADITIONAL VS. ROTH SELF-DIRECTED IRA

- **Traditional SDIRA:** Contributions are tax-deductible today, grow tax-deferred, and are taxed when withdrawn in retirement.
- **Roth SDIRA:** Contributions are made with after-tax dollars (no deduction today), but growth and withdrawals in retirement are completely tax-free.

Here's how I've structured it with my own family: instead of just paying taxes on every dollar of profit that flows through the management company, I allocate a portion of that income toward my spouse's self-directed IRA. Instead of my spouse's IRA sitting in the stock market with little control, it's invested in assets we choose, often in deals we're already working on. The contribution is deductible to the business, which reduces our taxable income today. At the same time, the funds grow inside a retirement account where compounding can do its magic year after year. So why does an SDIRA make sense for your spouse:

1. Tax-Free Growth Forever

If your management company makes contributions to a Roth SDIRA for your spouse, every real estate deal or investment inside that account grows without future tax. This means rental income, appreciation, and profits from property sales held inside the Roth SDIRA are never taxed—even when withdrawn in retirement.

2. Best for Younger Spouses or Long Timelines

If your spouse is younger or you're planning decades ahead, the Roth is powerful because compounding works its magic tax-free over time.

3. Aligns With Your Real Estate Strategy

A Roth SDIRA allows investment in alternative assets like real estate, private placements, notes, or syndications—not just stocks. That means you can take what you know (real estate) and use it inside the account for exponential tax-free growth.

4. Estate Planning Advantage

Roth IRAs are also incredibly powerful for generational wealth. Because withdrawals are tax-free, inheriting beneficiaries (like your kids) can take distributions without getting crushed by income taxes.

The result? I'm not just lowering our tax bill in the current year. I'm also building another bucket of generational wealth that compounds outside of the business. By doing this through my spouse, I maximize household contributions while spreading out the tax benefits.

This is the mindset shift: when you run your life like a business, you don't just think about income—you think about where that income flows. Every dollar can either go to the IRS or be redirected into vehicles like a self-directed IRA, where it continues working for your family. For me, that's an easy choice.

I thought it was important to show you the difference between a traditional IRA and a Roth IRA:

For long-term wealth building, many investors prefer the Roth version over the traditional self-directed IRA.

Here's the balance to consider: If your goal is to reduce taxable income now, a traditional SDIRA gives you the deduction. If your goal is long-term tax-free wealth, a Roth SDIRA is the better move—even though you don't get the deduction today.

Some investors even "ladder" both—making deductible contributions in high-income years, then funding Roth accounts consistently for long-term compounding. You can do this in a Roth. The trade-off is no deduction today in exchange for tax-free growth forever. If you're serious about building multi-generational wealth, Roth SDIRAs for your spouse (and eventually your kids when they qualify) are one of the most powerful tools in the playbook.

When you're using a Self-Directed IRA—whether Traditional or Roth—the contribution rules are identical to those of standard IRAs. Here's what you need to know, but always check with your tax professional or legal tax strategist:

- **Under age 50:** You may contribute up to $7,000 per year.
- **Aged 50 and up:** You're eligible for a $1,000 catch-up, allowing total contributions of up to $8,000 annually.

These limits apply across all IRA accounts combined. Whether you're funding a traditional, Roth, or self-directed IRA, your total annual contributions cannot exceed these thresholds.

Income Eligibility for Roth SDIRA

If you're contributing to a Roth version of a Self-Directed IRA, your ability to contribute may be phased out based on your Modified Adjusted Gross Income (MAGI):

- Singles: Full contributions if MAGI is under $150,000. Phase-out begins at $150,000 and ends at $165,000.
- Married Filing Jointly: Full contributions if MAGI is under $236,000, with phase-outs between $236,000 and $246,000.

Traditional SDIRAs have no income-based contribution eligibility limits—you can contribute as long as you meet the standard thresholds. These are examples, again check for updates and changes in the regulations.

Quick Summary Table

Account Type	Contribution Limit	Additional Info
Traditional SDIRA	$7,000 (under 50) $8,000 (age 50+)	Deductible contributions; no income phase-out for contribution eligibility.
Roth SDIRA	$7,000 (under 50) $8,000 (age 50+)	After-tax contributions; tax-free growth and tax-free withdrawals in retirement. Contribution eligibility subject to income limits.

In closing, if your goal is long-term, tax-free growth—and you're inside the income limits—the Roth self-directed IRA is a powerful tool, especially when investing in real estate or alternative assets. Just remember, whether traditional or Roth, the annual limit remains $7K (or $8K if age 50+), and Roth eligibility depends on your income.

Here's how the math works if you consistently contribute the maximum $7,000/year into a Roth Self-Directed IRA at a 9% average annual return:

- **20 Years of Contributions**
  - Total invested: $140,000
  - Grows to: ≈ $358,000 (over $218,000 of growth)
- **30 Years of Contributions**
  - Total invested: $210,000
  - Grows to: ≈ $954,000 (over $744,000 of growth)

Every dollar you contribute compounds over time—and inside a Roth Self-Directed IRA, that nearly $1 million nest egg is 100% tax-free in retirement. No capital gains, no income tax, no IRS share of your hard work.

This is exactly why wealthy investors maximize Roth accounts whenever they can. It's not just about the annual deduction—it's about creating permanent tax-free income streams for yourself and even for your heirs.

Now do this for you and your spouse and look at what you both achieved, not mention what you achieved in your real estate portfolio:

Here's the projection if both you and your spouse contribute $14,000/year combined for twenty years and then stop, letting it compound untouched for another ten years at a 9% return:

After 20 Years of Contributions

- Total invested: $280,000
- Account value: ≈ $716,000

Letting It Grow 10 More Years (No Contributions)

- Account value at year 30: ≈ $1,696,000

This shows the raw power of compounding. Even if you stopped contributing after twenty years, the money you already invested nearly doubles in the next ten years without adding a single extra dollar.

Maximize income streams, keep expenses tight, and deliver more than the competition

---

That's why Roth self-directed IRAs are such a key piece of the wealth-building puzzle. You don't just save taxes today—you build a tax-free compounding machine that grows long after you stop feeding it.

VALUE-ADD: MASSIVELY INCREASING PROPERTY INCOME

The fastest way to grow income isn't always buying more buildings. Often, it's unlocking what's already there. Value-add investing rewards observation. Many properties are underperforming simply because no one ever questioned the status quo. Some of the most effective value-add strategies include:

- **Parking:** Often overlooked, frequently underpriced
- **Garages:** Small rents compound quickly
- **Laundry:** Low capital, high margin
- **Storage:** Monetize unused space
- **ADUs:** Turn square footage into doors
- **Utilities:** Shift costs appropriately

Every improvement increases NOI. And every dollar of NOI multiplies property value. When I walk a property, I don't just see walls, roofs, and units. I see opportunities. Every inch of a building is a chance to increase value through higher rent, added services, or reduced expenses. My philosophy is simple: maximize income streams, keep expenses tight, and deliver more than the competition.

Value-add investing rewards observation

Parking

One of the first things I evaluate is parking. Most landlords ignore it or toss it in for free. Not me. Parking is a service. It has costs—snow removal, striping, repairs—so why shouldn't it also generate revenue?

Here's my system:

- Every tenant gets an assigned space, clearly numbered.
- I issue a matching placard for the tenant's car. No placard = no parking.
- I would check your area for competitive pricing for parking.

And I enforce it. I have arrangements with towing companies for illegal parking. My leases include a clause. If rent isn't paid, parking privileges are revoked. Nothing motivates tenants faster than circling the block for street parking. That single move—treating parking as an asset—adds thousands of dollars a year to my bottom line and, more importantly, increases the property's cap rate and overall value.

Garages

Some properties come with garages, which can be even more lucrative. I rent them for market value, either to tenants or outside renters. They're basic—just space, a lightbulb, maybe some outlets—but people pay. Still, garages can come with surprises. I joke that I own "the most famous garage in town." Here's why:

Round 1: Exotic Alligators

My first garage tenant seemed harmless. During inspections, the space looked fine. Months later, I got a call from the chief of police, with whom I happened to play poker with. "Glenn, we need into your garage on Tyler Ave. We have a warrant." I drilled the lock, opened the door, and found 150 breeding tanks full of exotic alligators. It made the front page of the paper.

Round 2: The Chop Shop

The next tenant was a mechanic at Toyota. Verified job, solid references. Safe bet, right? Wrong. Same call from the chief, same drill. Inside: shelves stacked with stripped car electronics. He was involved in a chop shop. I was part of another front-page story.

Round 3: The Snapple Machines

This one looked even better. I had a guy storing vending machines. Just boxes and machines stacked floor to ceiling. It seemed harmless. That is, until the police raided. Turns out he was moving drugs inside the machines. Once again, my garage made the local paper.

After three fiascos, I thought I was cursed. Finally, a retired cop rented the garage for his classic cars. Best tenant I ever had.

The lesson is to treat garages like apartments. Screen tenants, inspect regularly, and put clear restrictions in the lease. And know, even with background checks and references, issues can occur.

Laundry

Another gold mine is coin-operated laundry facilities. For buildings with eight or more units, I always install a laundry room. Below that, it doesn't pay. And I never allow individual machines in smaller units. They leak, waste water, and destroy floors.

Years ago, my water bill spiked for three months straight. Turns out one tenant had turned her apartment into a neighborhood laundromat, running machines day and night—all on my dime. That ended quickly.

Now my policy is strict. I cover cold water only. Tenants pay for hot water use. I remove all outdoor hose bibs so tenants can't wash cars or set up kiddie pools. I install coin- or card-operated laundry machines where feasible. These machines don't just cover costs. They generate a steady income and provide tenants with a valued amenity. It's one of the easiest wins in real estate.

Storage Units

Basements are goldmines most landlords waste. I build 6 x 6 storage cages and rent them for $35–$55 per month. Tenants love the convenience of bikes, holiday decorations, or boxes of stuff they don't want upstairs.

It may not sound like much, but in a ten-unit building with six rented lockers at $40 per month, that's $2,880 a year of pure profit—and it increases the building's cap rate.

Accessory Dwelling Units

In some states, especially California, accessory dwelling units (ADUs) are game changers. With the right permits, you can legally convert garages, basements, or rear structures into new apartments.

My nephew Ben has mastered this. He hunts for triplexes or fourplexes with big garages and converts them into two- or three-bedroom apartments. It's not easy—permits, inspections, red tape—but the payoff is massive. One conversion can add hundreds of thousands of dollars in value. More importantly, watching Ben run with this idea has been one of my proudest moments. He's proof that the system I've built can be taught, adapted, and scaled.

Mentoring him reminds me why I wrote this book: not just to share stories, but to give a roadmap that others can follow.

Value-add is not speculation. Its execution.

THE BRRRR METHOD

BRRRR—Buy, Rehab, Rent, Refinance, Repeat—has become a buzzword. When done well, it works. When rushed, it destroys portfolios. My view is intentionally conservative:

- Buy with margin
- Rehab with discipline
- Rent realistically
- Refinance cautiously
- Repeat only when systems are ready

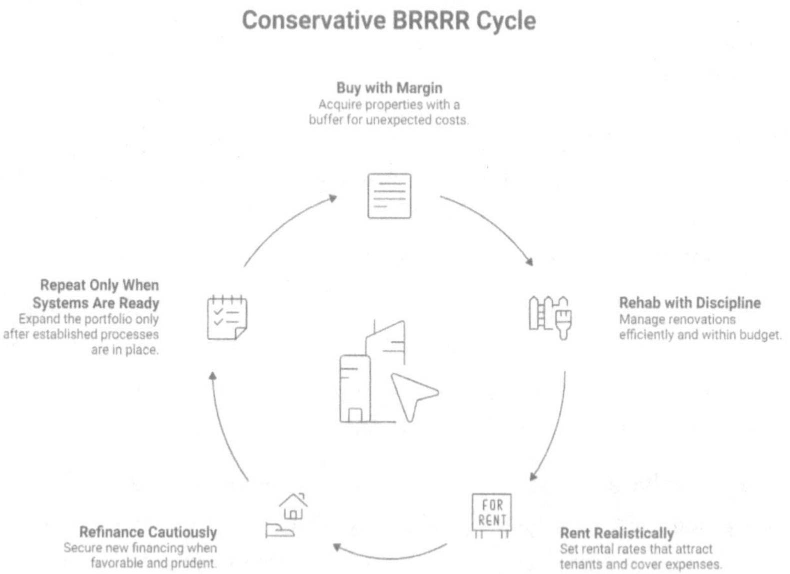

The mistake people make is treating BRRRR like a shortcut. It isn't. It's a multiplier. Multipliers amplify discipline, and they amplify mistakes.

The beauty of BRRRR is leverage. You buy once, add value, and then pull out much of your original capital—often tax-free—while keeping the cash-flowing asset. Done right, each cycle accelerates your path to financial freedom. Done wrong, it ties up cash, creates sleepless nights, and can stall your entire investing career.

Now let's break down each stage of the process with the exact filters, metrics, and field lessons I use to make sure every deal is worth the risk.

Step 1 – Buy

When using the BRRRR method, I never rush to buy. I use my analyzer tool and stay strict to the formula. I fell in love with the deal, not the property. Remember, this is an *investment* property, not a home for your family.

An ideal BRRRR property needs moderate repairs. Look for homes that are undervalued in a strong neighborhood and have solid comparable sales (comps).

Avoid shiny turnkey listings that have already been fully renovated. You will pay retail and leave no room to force appreciation. On the other extreme, steer clear of total gut jobs unless you already run a construction crew. Complete teardowns can eat both time and profit.

My sweet spot is to find houses that need paint, updated kitchens or baths, and new flooring. Basically, I'm looking for improvements that boost value without blowing the budget. And always remember my location rule. You must feel comfortable visiting the property at 2 a.m.

Most first-phase investors use conventional financing—20–30% down with a standard mortgage, or a DSCR (Debt Service Coverage Ratio) loan. Review the financing options in Chapter 3 to pick what fits your capital and risk tolerance. I love the house hack method to start.

Step 2 – Rehab

The goal of rehab is two-fold: (1) maximize income and increase property value. And (2) line up contractors and a timeline before you close, so work begins immediately. Focus on updates with the highest ROI: kitchens, bathrooms, flooring, and a clean, modern paint job.

Efficiency is everything. Time is money, so work only with reliable contractors and be present. Ask questions, learn their process, and keep detailed records. Never pay in untracked cash. Collect invoices and W-9s for every vendor so you're ready for year-end 1099s.

Don't overlook mechanics. Service boilers, flush water heaters, and replace worn faucets or toilets. Most late-night calls come from heat and water issues, so tackle those first.

Step 3 – Rent

Once rehab is complete, set the right rent using tools like Rentometer, Zillow, and Apartments.com to compare similar units. Pricing accurately does two things: it increases cash flow *and* proves to lenders you understand the market.

Follow the screening process from chapter 5: verify income, credit, and references, and don't forget the car test. Require at least 1.5 months' worth of rest for a security deposit plus the first month's rent. Collect it in cash or certified funds at move-in. Solid tenants mean fewer headaches and stronger refinance appraisals.

Step 4 – Refinance

Here's where BRRRR shines. With repairs done and rents up, your property is now worth more. Suppose you bought for $600k, invested $150k in rehab, and the new appraisal comes in at $900k. You can refinance based on that higher value, pull out much of your initial cash tax-free, and still own a property that provides positive cash flow.

Step 5 – Repeat

Use the capital from your refinance to buy the next property and start again. Each cycle builds experience, equity, and cash flow. You can move from a Phase-1 investor (a handful of properties) to a Phase-2 investor (running a scalable business with a team and private capital).

When you have a track record and fifteen-plus doors, you're no longer just "buying rentals." You're operating a portfolio with systems, credibility, and leverage to raise funds and grow exponentially.

I pulled off a neat little trick with Home Depot that helped me finance a big chunk of the renovations. I went straight to the Pro Desk at my local store, opened a Home Depot credit card, and worked out a deal where I could access $150,000 in credit interest-free, with no payments due for twelve months. That was essentially free money for a year, and I took full advantage. I bought every supply I needed for the renovation through Home Depot, completed the project in about seven months, then refinanced the property, which took another three months. With the refinance funds, I paid the card off a week before the twelve-month cycle ended, avoiding every penny of interest. That's what I call a win-win: I got the building renovated, built equity, boosted cash flow, and used Home Depot's line of credit without paying them a dime in interest. Winner winner chicken dinner!

BRRRR works when you treat it like a professional playbook, not a weekend hobby.

Analyze ruthlessly, rehab efficiently, screen tenants carefully, and refinance strategically. Execute with discipline, and you'll build a flywheel of assets that can fund your next deal—and your financial freedom—for decades. At this stage, you've learned how to build, protect, and scale assets. What remains is not strategy, it's continuity.

In the next chapter, we move beyond wealth and into permanence: how to transfer knowledge, values, and opportunity so that what you build outlives you.

CHAPTER 8
GENERATIONAL WEALTH SYSTEMS

Now, I'm going to be critical of you and ask you to be critical of yourself. You need to change your approach, change your thinking, because society has brainwashed you.

I'll never forget when this finally clicked for me. Once it made sense, I wasn't just surprised—I was furious. Why didn't my accountant teach me this? Why did I spend years believing the system was built to take care of me when really the system is designed to keep me working, paying taxes, and staying average?

The truth is, most accountants just crank out tax returns. They like simplicity; they want to fill the right boxes and then move on. They aren't trained or incentivized to help you build wealth.

When I finally hired a tax strategist and devoured book after book on taxes, investing, and wealth, the lightbulb didn't just turn on; it exploded. And with it came anger. How could I have been so blind? Why couldn't I see the forest through the trees? Why did I earn a master's degree from USC and still feel financially ignorant? I blamed my parents. I blamed my accountant. I blamed the school system. But at the end of the day, I had to stop blaming everyone else. I had to take responsibility for my own life and my own financial education.

That's when the shift happened. My mindset flipped from anger and blame to ownership and opportunity. I realized I figured it out. And 99% of people still haven't. From that day forward, I committed to treating my life like a business. Every day, every decision, every dollar. My household isn't just a family, it's a corporation with rules, systems, and long-term strategies.

That shift is what gave me financial independence. Freedom. The ability to do what I want when I want. And that's the mindset I'm passing down to my family.

If I could give the next generation one advantage, it wouldn't be money. It would be positioning.

Most young adults are taught to buy a starter home—a place to live, decorate, and eventually outgrow. Very few are taught to buy a starter asset.

First-time homebuyer programs quietly provide one of the greatest leverage opportunities available, especially when paired with small multi-family properties. These programs typically offer:

- Lower down payments
- Favorable interest rates
- Owner-occupied flexibility
- Reduced qualification hurdles

When combined with a one- to four-unit property, something powerful happens. Housing stops being a cost and starts becoming a contributor. A young buyer can live in one unit while tenants cover much or all of the mortgage. Equity builds. Confidence grows. Financial literacy accelerates. This isn't about gaming the system. It's about using the system as intended. Most people miss this window because no one explains it to them in time.

WHY FINANCIAL LITERACY MATTERS (ESPECIALLY FOR FAMILIES)

If you don't understand the rules of money, you'll always play someone else's game. And in that game, you're designed to lose. Schools teach you how to be an employee, not an owner. Accountants teach you how to follow forms, not build wealth. Banks teach you how to borrow, not how to leverage. And employers teach you how to work harder, not smarter.

The truth is wealth isn't about how much you earn; it's about how much you keep, multiply, and protect. That's why financial literacy isn't optional. It's a survival skill. And if you don't pass it on to your kids, they'll inherit your properties but not your mindset. They'll sell, squander, and lose the very thing you spent a lifetime building.

THE ESSENTIAL PILLARS

Over the years, complexity stripped itself away. After enough deals, enough mistakes, and enough reflection, only a few principles remained.

These became my non-negotiables—the Four Musts.

1. **Cash Flow First**
2. Appreciation is unpredictable. Cash flow creates control. If a deal doesn't pay you, it owns you.
3. **Fixed Debt Wins**
4. Predictability beats cleverness. Adjustable risk compounds quietly.
5. **Systems Over Talent**
6. Talent disappears. Systems endure. If it can't run without you, it won't outlive you.
7. **Family Always Comes First**
8. Wealth without values fractures families. Assets should serve people, not replace them.

Every decision I make filters through these pillars. If one fails, the deal fails. These principles don't just guide investments; they guide behavior.

FINANCIAL EDUCATION FOR THE FAMILY

Money habits are not inherited. They are taught or neglected. One of my strongest convictions is that financial education belongs at home, long before adulthood, and not with lectures and pressure But with exposure. Children don't need complexity. They need context. Our family education framework focuses on five areas:

1. **Mindset:** delayed gratification, ownership, responsibility
2. **Money:** earning, saving, investing
3. **Taxes:** why structure matters
4. **Real Estate:** assets, leverage, systems
5. **Decision-Making:** consequences and tradeoffs

We talk openly. We explain decisions. We show, not just tell. The goal is not entitlement. It's competence.

BUILDING GENERATIONAL WEALTH THROUGH LIFE INSURANCE

For most of my life, I thought life insurance was just a grim necessity, a policy you buy to protect your family if something happens to you. It was something my financial advisor pushed on me early in my career, and I dutifully signed up for a term policy to cover the mortgage and provide for Theresa and the kids if I wasn't around. It felt like a check-box: pay the premium, forget about it, hope you never need it. After acquiring my first few multi-family properties, I started to think about taxes, legacy, and long-term security, and I had a revelation. Life insurance isn't just about death. Done right, it's a living tool. It's a way to build tax-advantaged wealth; protect your assets from creditors and lawsuits; shield your estate from crippling taxes; and even generate supplemental, tax-free income during your lifetime. It became the missing piece in my financial puzzle, complementing my real estate investments like a perfectly matched set of gears. I remember the exact moment it clicked. I was going over how to structure my trusts to minimize estate taxes with my estate planner. He casually mentioned using life insurance not just for the death benefit but as a "family bank" where I could borrow against the cash value tax-free to fund real estate deals or supplement retirement income. My jaw dropped. Why hadn't anyone told me this sooner? If I had started in my twenties, I could have compounded even more wealth. But like everything in this book, better late than never. I dove in, restructured my policies, and now life insurance is a cornerstone of my plan, not just for protection but for growth and income. In this chapter, I'll break down how life insurance serves as a powerhouse for asset and estate protection, how it can provide supplemental tax-free income while you're alive, and the game-changing benefits of incorporating it into your wealth-building strategy. This isn't theory; it's what I've lived and implemented. If you're building wealth through real estate or any other means, ignoring life insurance is like leaving money on the table and exposing your hard-earned assets to unnecessary risks.

Types of Life Insurance

Before we get into the advanced strategies, let's define the landscape. There are two main categories of life insurance: term and permanent.

Term Life Insurance is the simple, affordable kind—pure protection. You pay premiums for a set period (say, twenty or thirty years), and if you die during that term, your beneficiaries get the death benefit. No cash value builds up; it's like renting insurance. I used the term early on to cover my family while I was grinding in corporate America and building my real estate portfolio. It's great for short-term needs, but it expires worthless if you outlive the term.

Permanent Life Insurance: This is where the magic happens. Policies like whole life, universal life (UL), indexed universal life (IUL), or variable universal life (VUL) provide lifelong coverage as long as you pay premiums. More importantly, they build cash value over time. A portion of your premium goes into a savings-like component that grows tax-deferred. This cash value is what turns life insurance from a death benefit into a living benefit. I shifted to permanent policies—specifically, IULs—once my real estate cash flow stabilized. Why? Because the cash value grows based on market indexes (like the S&P 500) with downside protection (floors to prevent losses), and I can access it without triggering taxes. It's like a Roth IRA on steroids, but without contribution limits. If you're young and starting, prioritize permanent policies early; the compounding is unbeatable.

Asset and Estate Protection

One of the most underrated roles of life insurance is protection. In a world full of uncertainties—lawsuits, market crashes, health crises, or even divorce—life insurance acts as a shield for your assets and estate. Here's how:

Creditor and Lawsuit Protection

Real estate investors like us are prime targets for lawsuits. A tenant slips on ice, a contractor botches a job, or a car accident turns litigious, and suddenly your properties and savings are at risk. But the cash value of a life insurance policy and death benefits are often protected from creditors in most states. (Check your local laws. Some states offer unlimited protection, others cap it. For example, early in my portfolio-building days, I faced a frivolous lawsuit from a tenant claiming mold issues. (It was user error, but that's another story.) My attorney pointed out that my life insurance policies were untouchable. That gave me peace of mind while we fought it out. Had I kept that money in a taxable brokerage account, it could have been frozen or seized. Now I know to structure my policies in an irrevocable life insurance trust (ILIT) for even stronger protection. Creditors can't touch what's owned by the trust.

Estate Tax Shield

Estate taxes can decimate your legacy. As of the beginning of 2026, the federal estate tax exemption was $15 million. Anything above that gets taxed at up to 40%. For families with substantial real estate portfolios, this is a killer. Life insurance protects your assets by providing tax-free liquidity to pay estate taxes without forcing a fire sale of assets. The death benefit goes straight to beneficiaries (or the trust) income-tax-free. In my setup, my ILIT owns the policies, so the death benefit isn't even part of my taxable estate. It's like creating money out of thin air to cover Uncle Sam's bill. Without it, my heirs might have to sell a multi-family building at a bad time just to pay taxes. With it, the properties stay in the family, continuing to generate income.

Divorce and Family Protection

Life gets messy. In a divorce, assets can be split, but life insurance in a trust often stays protected (especially if it's set up before the marriage). It ensures your intended beneficiaries—kids or grandkids—get the benefit, not an ex-spouse or your child's ex, who thinks they will get access to the family wealth. I also use it to equalize inheritances. If one child gets the family business, another might get a larger life insurance payout to balance things out.

Business Continuity

As my real estate grew into a business, I added key-person insurance on myself. If something happens to me, the policy pays out to cover transition costs, buy out partners, or keep operations running. It's cheap protection for a high-stakes game.

Permanent Policies as Tax-Free Income

This blew my mind. Life insurance isn't just for after you're gone. Permanent policies can provide supplemental, tax-free income while you're alive, acting as a personal ATM for retirement, emergencies, or opportunities. The living benefits or permanent policies changed my game. This is where cash value shines.

Building and Accessing Cash Value

In a permanent policy, part of your premium funds the death benefit, and the rest goes into cash value. This grows tax-deferred at a guaranteed growth or 3–5%. IUL ties to indexes with floors (0% minimum, caps around 10-12%), VUL invests in markets for higher potential but more risk. Over time, cash value accumulates like a high-yield savings account on steroids. The key is withdrawing it could trigger taxes, but borrowing against it is tax-free, with low interest (often 4–6%, charged against the policy). As long as the policy stays in force, you never have to repay the loan; it's deducted from the death benefit later. In my case, I funded an IUL aggressively. I can borrow, for example, $200,000 tax-free from my policy to fund a down payment on a new multi-family deal. There is no bank approval, no income verification, just quick liquidity. The policy keeps growing on the full cash value (loans don't stop compounding), and the interest was offset by the policy's growth.

Supplemental Income in Retirement

Imagine retiring with real estate cash flow, Social Security, and a tax-free stream from life insurance. Many people overfund policies (up to IRS limits to avoid modified endowment contract status) to maximize cash value. In retirement, you can take annual loans—say, $150,000/year tax-free—to supplement income without dipping into taxable accounts like 401(k)s or IRAs. The benefits are that there are no required minimum distributions (RMDs) like retirement accounts, so you control the timing. Loans don't count as income, so they don't push you into higher tax brackets or affect Social Security taxation. For me, this means more spendable money in retirement without IRS penalties.

Emergency Fund or Opportunity Capital

Life throws curveballs—medical bills, market dips, or a killer real estate deal. Cash value loans provide instant access without selling assets at a loss. During the 2020 COVID dip, I borrowed against my policy to scoop up a distressed property. The loan rate was lower than a HELOC, and it was tax-free. Win-win.

Tax Advantages Over Other Vehicles

Compared to a Roth IRA (with limited contributions), life insurance has no income limits or caps. You can pour in as much as the policy allows. Growth is tax-deferred, access is tax-free, and death benefits are tax-free. It's like a super-Roth for high earners.

Here are the key benefits:

Tax Efficiency: Everything about it screams tax savings—deferred growth, tax-free loans, tax-free death benefit. In a world where taxes eat 30–50% of gains, this is huge. My real estate provides depreciation deductions; life insurance adds another layer of tax sheltering.

Liquidity and Flexibility: Unlike locked-up retirement accounts or illiquid real estate, cash value is accessible anytime. No early withdrawal penalties (pre-59½ like IRAs). It's your money on your terms.

Downside Protection and Growth Potential: IULs protect against market losses (0% floor) while capturing upside. In volatile times, this beats straight stock investing. My policy has averaged 7–8% growth, compounding tax-free.

Legacy Amplification: The death benefit replenishes what you borrow, ensuring heirs get a full payout. It's like spending money that regenerates. Combined with trusts, it creates perpetual wealth.

Peace of Mind: Knowing my family is protected, my estate taxes covered, and I have a tax-free income stream—priceless. It lets me sleep at night and take calculated risks in real estate.

Inflation Hedge: Cash value growth often outpaces inflation, preserving purchasing power. Loans let you access it without eroding the base.

No Contribution Limits for High Earners: If you are maxing out 401(k)s and IRAs, life insurance is the next bucket. I overfund mine annually, turning excess income into tax-advantaged wealth.

Integration with Real Estate: Use loans for down payments, rehabs, or bridging gaps in cash flow. It's leverage without traditional debt, which is perfect for scaling your portfolio.

Pitfalls and Tips: How to Do It Right

- **Avoid Overfunding:** Stay under modified endowment contract (MEC) limits, or loans become taxable.
- **Shop Carriers:** Not all policies are equal. You should compare crediting rates, fees, and guarantees.
- **Work with Pros:** A good advisor (not a salesman) designs your estate for your goals. I use an independent advisor who has been in this business for a long time.
- **Start Early:** Compounding needs time. A twenty-five-year-old policy could have 10x the cash value by sixty-five.
- **Annual Reviews:** Monitor loans, growth, and health to keep it optimized.
- **Costs:** Permanent policies have higher premiums than term—view it as an investment, not an expense.

A while back, I needed $150,000 for a property upgrade. Instead of a bank loan (with underwriting and interest), I borrowed from my IUL. The loan was tax-free and quick, and the policy grew anyway. That upgrade boosted rents 20%, paying for itself in no time. Now, in semi-retirement, I take $40,000/year tax-free to travel all without touching the principal. It's freedom.

Life insurance isn't just protection. It's a multifaceted tool for wealth building. It safeguards your assets and estate while providing tax-free income to live your best life today. Integrate it with your real estate strategy, and you'll create a powerhouse system. Don't wait; start building your policy today. Your future self—and your heirs—will thank you.

Life insurance doesn't replace real estate. It stabilizes it.

THE FAMILY CONSTITUTION

When most people think about wealth, they picture dollar signs, bank accounts, and properties. But I've learned that money without structure doesn't just disappear; it destroys families. I've seen it with my own eyes. Families who built empires lost it all within a generation or two because there were no rules, no system, no constitution holding everything together.

Here's the hard truth: wealth can divide just as quickly as it can unite. Without a plan, inheritances become lawsuits, siblings turn into enemies, and the legacy you worked your entire life to build gets burned to the ground by the very people you built it for. That's why I created a family constitution. For me, this wasn't about creating some fancy document to hang on the wall. It was about creating a living guide, a rule book for how my family will steward *our* wealth, protect *our* values, and carry *our* legacy forward.

I wanted to make sure my kids and their kids after them don't just inherit real estate, life insurance, or trust distributions. I want them to inherit a framework that teaches them responsibility, demands contribution, and ensures fairness. Because here's the reality: if you don't write the rules, the rules will be written for you by the courts, by the IRS, or by family conflict.

The family constitution isn't about control. It's about clarity. It says: This is who we are. This is how we manage our wealth. This is how we resolve conflicts. And this is how we make sure that what we worked for doesn't end up gone in three generations.

Think of it like the foundation of a building. Without it, no matter how tall you build, the structure eventually collapses. With it, you can keep adding floors, expanding, and improving for generations. Building wealth is one thing. Protecting it and passing it down responsibly is another.

Most families never talk about money until it creates conflict. Most families fall apart when money enters the picture. Siblings fight. In-laws push for influence. Children grow up entitled. Without structure, wealth divides more than it unites.

A trust and a portfolio of real estate will secure your family financially. Without rules, vision, and accountability, even the strongest fortune can be squandered. A family constitution ensures that doesn't happen. It's not a legal document like a trust (though the two work hand in hand). It's a guiding framework—a charter—that every generation can look to for direction.

In this chapter, I walk you through what a family constitution looks like, how to create one, and most importantly, why you cannot afford to ignore it.

A family constitution protects your assets from the problems I just mentioned by:

- **Defining values** – hard work, persistence, education, giving back.
- **Setting expectations** – who can access resources, under what conditions.
- **Preserving legacy** – ensuring your name and mission carry forward for generations.
- **Preventing disputes** – setting clear. rules to minimize arguments.

This is about more than wealth. It's about culture. You're not just leaving assets; you're leaving a way of life.

KEY ELEMENTS OF A FAMILY CONSTITUTION

1. Mission Statement

Every constitution starts answers the question why. Why are we doing this? What does your family stand for? What is the purpose of this wealth? For me, it's simple: to create financial security and opportunity for my children and grandchildren while instilling in them a sense of responsibility, discipline, and contribution to society.

2. Core Values

These are non-negotiables. In my constitution, we emphasize:

- **Work ethic** – nothing is given without effort.
- **Education** – whether college or trade, continuous learning is required.
- **Financial literacy** – heirs must understand money before managing it.
- **Contribution** – giving to family, to community, and to future generations is important.

3. Governance Structure

Who makes decisions? The trust has a trustee, but the constitution may establish a family council or board of advisors that includes family members and, in some cases, outside professionals. This creates accountability by preventing one person from holding all the power.

4. Rules for Participation

- No "trust fund babies." Benefits are earned, not handed out.
- Family members must be employed, educated, or contributing meaningfully to access trust benefits.
- Loans from the family bank (via life insurance cash value) require approval and a repayment plan, even if repayment comes at death.

5. Philanthropy & Giving

We embed giving into the constitution. A percentage of trust income is earmarked for charity every year. This keeps the family humble and reminds future generations that wealth comes with responsibility.

6. Conflict Resolution

Disagreements are inevitable. The constitution should define how they're handled, generally through mediation, arbitration, or majority vote by the family council. This keeps disputes from destroying relationships.

7. Succession & Continuity

Every constitution must answer what happens when the current leaders are gone. By clearly outlining succession, you avoid power struggles and confusion.

THE CONSTITUTION IN ACTION

Here's how it works in real life. Say one of my grandchildren wants to borrow from the family bank for a business idea. The constitution requires:

- A written business plan.
- Review by the family council.
- Proof of financial literacy (courses completed).
- Agreement that funds are deducted from future inheritance if unpaid.

If they meet those requirements, they get support. If not, they don't. It's not about saying no; it's about teaching responsibility.

The constitution transforms wealth from a pile of assets into a living system. It keeps the family aligned, instills discipline, and avoids the "shirtsleeves to shirtsleeves in three generations" curse. This proverb describes how wealth built by the first generation (shirtsleeves) is often lost by the third, returning to poverty (shirtsleeves again) due to lack of financial planning, entitlement, and understanding of wealth creation. I want my family not just to be wealthy but to be strong, united, and purposeful. The family constitution is the glue that holds all of this together.

If you've come this far—building assets, structuring trusts, setting up the family bank—don't skip this step. A family constitution is the playbook that ensures your legacy isn't wasted. It tells your heirs not just what they're inheriting, but how to steward it. Without this rule book, money can destroy. With it, money can empower. And that, to me, is the true definition of generational wealth.

SAMPLE FAMILY CONSTITUTION: PREAMBLE

We, the [Family Name] Family, believe that our wealth is not only a financial asset but also a responsibility. It is our duty to protect, preserve, and grow this wealth for future generations, while instilling values of hard work, education, and contribution to society. This Constitution shall serve as our guiding framework for governance, stewardship, and legacy.

1. Mission Statement

Our mission is to ensure financial security for our family members, to provide opportunities for education and enterprise, and to foster unity, discipline, and contribution. We commit to building wealth that endures for generations and to using that wealth responsibly to better ourselves, our community, and the world.

2. Core Values

- **Work Ethic:** Nothing is given without effort. Every family member is expected to contribute meaningfully through work, study, or service.
- **Education:** Lifelong learning—whether academic, vocational, or entrepreneurial—is a requirement for participation in family wealth.
- **Financial Literacy:** All heirs must demonstrate understanding of budgeting, investing, and wealth stewardship before accessing significant resources.

- **Contribution:** Each member must contribute to the family, the community, or society at large to benefit from family resources.
- **Integrity:** Decisions must be made honestly, transparently, and in alignment with our mission.

3. Governance Structure

- **Trustee(s):** Appointed professionals or family members responsible for managing the trust and enforcing its terms.
- **Family Council:** A group of family members (and advisors, if necessary) who meet at least annually to review assets, vote on major decisions, and discuss family matters.
- **Board of Advisors (optional):** Non-family professionals (attorneys, accountants, or trusted mentors) who provide guidance and oversight.

4. Participation Rules

- No trust fund babies. Distributions are earned, not automatic.
- Family members must be employed, pursuing education, or contributing in a meaningful way to access benefits.
- Access to the Family Bank (loans from life insurance or trust assets) requires:
    - Written request and purpose (business, education, first home).
    - Review and approval by the Family Council.
    - Agreement that borrowed amounts reduce future inheritance if not repaid.

5. Philanthropy and Giving

- A minimum of [X]% of annual trust income shall be allocated to charitable causes approved by the Family Council.
- Charitable giving shall reflect our family's values in education, health, and community development.

- Each generation is encouraged to identify and support causes that matter to them, keeping generosity at the heart of our legacy.

6. Conflict Resolution

- Any disputes regarding family assets, trust distributions, or Constitution rules will go to mediation first.
- If unresolved by mediation, disputes will be decided by arbitration, binding upon all parties.
- Family unity takes priority over personal disagreements.

7. Succession and Continuity

- Succession planning must always be in place for Trustees, Family Council members, and Business Managers.
- Each generation shall appoint and train the next to take on leadership roles.
- Annual retreats and educational workshops will ensure continuity of knowledge and values.

8. Lifestyle and Discipline

- Family members are encouraged to live within their means and avoid excessive lifestyles that put wealth or reputation at risk.
- Major purchases (luxury homes, cars, etc.) should not exceed sustainable financial limits and must not require family trust resources.
- The Constitution emphasizes building assets before acquiring liabilities.

9. Amendments

This Constitution may be amended only by a [two-thirds / unanimous] vote of the Family Council, ensuring flexibility for future generations while protecting the founding vision.

Closing Statement

We recognize that wealth without responsibility divides, but wealth with structure and values unites. This Family Constitution is both our shield and our compass. It will protect our family, guide our decisions, and ensure that the fruits of our labor endure for generations to come.

Signed this day,

[Founders' Names]

[Date]

TRUSTS & LEGACY STRUCTURES

When it comes to protecting everything you've worked for, nothing is more important than getting your legal structures in order. I can tell you firsthand, it's not quick, and it's not simple. It took me nearly a year to finalize my two trusts, my wills, and my health directives. But when it was done, the sense of relief was enormous. I knew that no matter what happened to me, my family would be protected, my wishes would be honored, and my wealth would pass on exactly the way I intended.

A trust isn't just a place to hold assets. It's a way to organize your entire financial life into a clear, enforceable system.

Most people put this off, thinking they'll get to it later. Don't! Life doesn't always give you the luxury of time, and procrastination here can cost your family dearly. Spend the time, invest in the right advisors, and be done with it. Once you have your structure in place, you'll wonder why you didn't do it sooner.

For me, I built two pillars into my estate plan. My revocable trust holds all of my real estate—flexible, amendable, and fully under my control while I'm alive. Alongside it, I created an irrevocable family legacy trust, which owns my life insurance and serves as the backbone of my generational wealth strategy. Together, these two trusts give me both flexibility today and protection for tomorrow. They are the playbook for my family: a system that eliminates confusion, avoids court interference, and ensures fairness across generations.

Here's what I've learned: the bigger your estate, the more moving parts there are. And the more moving parts, the greater the risk of confusion, conflict, and unnecessary taxes. A trust isn't just a place to hold assets. It's a way to organize your entire financial life into a clear, enforceable system. It tells the courts to stay out, it tells the IRS where the lines are drawn, and it tells your family exactly how to handle everything when you're no longer here to explain it yourself. For me, trusts were the difference between simply *owning* assets and truly *protecting* a legacy.

Now, my wife thinks I'm a little over the top with trusts and legacy structures. But I've seen how fast everything can turn upside down, and I know I did the right thing. Like everything else in this book, it comes down to protecting what you've built so the wealth you've worked so hard for isn't ripped out of the family.

A close friend of mine went from millionaire to bartender almost overnight. She made Wall Street money, lived in a McMansion, had the luxury cars, the whole package. But her husband was a financial liability. After a messy divorce, she was forced to give him half of everything. On top of that, her job performance slipped under stress, and she was let go. The cars went, the house went, and now she's bartending just to survive. Why? Because there was no planning. No trust. No asset protection. No insurance is structured the right way. One storm, and the entire empire collapsed.

That's why I'm obsessive about this. It's not paranoia; it's protection. Trusts, insurance, and estate planning aren't about today's comfort; they're about ensuring tomorrow's survival.

Real estate and life insurance are the engines of generational wealth. Trusts are the steering wheel. Without them, the car still moves, but it can drift, crash, or be taken by someone else. With the right trust structure, you control direction, protect passengers, and make sure the trip continues long after you're not the one driving.

Below is what each trust does, how they work together, and how to avoid the landmines that blow up most plans.

1) Revocable Living Trust (RLT)

Flexible Control + Probate Avoidance

An RLT is a will you can use while you're alive. You (the grantor) can amend or revoke it anytime. You're usually your own trustee first; a successor trustee takes over if you're incapacitated or when you pass. With an RLT, you will

- **Avoid probate.** Your heirs don't wait on a judge or pay court fees to transfer property.
- **Keep things private.** Wills are public; trusts aren't.
- **Step-Up in Basis.** Assets inside your RLT are typically included in your estate at death—so your heirs get a step-up in tax basis to fair market value on that date. For appreciated real estate, that's huge.

The best uses for an RLT (what I put here) include:

- All rental properties (titled into the trust via the deed).
- Operating/holding LLC membership interests (the trust owns the LLC; the LLC owns the property).
- Bank/brokerage accounts (retitled to the trust).
- A pour-over will to catch anything you forget to retitle and "pour it over" into the trust at death.

During your life, an RLT is a grantor trust—ignored for income tax. You file taxes as you do now.

Key Mechanics

- Successor trustees named (primary + backups).
- Distributions: simple "who gets what, when, and how."
- Disability provisions: how bills get paid and who can act if you're incapacitated.

RLTs do not protect your assets from your own creditors during your life (it's revocable), and it does not remove assets from your taxable estate. That's where the next structure comes in.

2) Irrevocable Life Insurance Trust (ILIT)

Protection + Perpetual Fuel

An IFLT is a separate, locked box you cannot change on a whim. Mine owns the life insurance that powers our family bank. Heirs benefit but do not own the assets, which is the protection magic. The primary objectives are to

- Keep death benefits outside your taxable estate.
- Provide lawsuit/divorce/creditor protection for heirs.
- Enforce rules (your Family Constitution) with trustee oversight.

The best uses for an ILIT (what I put here) include:

- Indexed/whole life policies (including premium-financed policies).
- A ruleset for loans/distributions (education, first home, business seed capital), not lifestyle burn.

. . .

There are several ways to fund an ILIT, including with

- **Annual gifts**—Be mindful of gift/estate tax limits; use Crummey notices if needed so gifts qualify for the annual exclusion. Beneficiaries must receive (and the trustee must document) withdrawal rights notices.
- **Premium financing**—A lender funds the premiums. Your policy and/or other collateral secures the loan; repayment often comes from death proceeds.
- **Policy loans** to beneficiaries under trustee guidelines. Remember, with policy loans, there are no bank approvals; it's not taxable income.

Properly drafted/operated, ILIT assets are outside your estate. There is no step-up in basis on assets placed into or owned by an ILIT. (That's why I keep appreciating real estate in the RLT/LLC lane and insurance in the ILIT lane.) ILITs hit compressed income-tax brackets fast; a well-designed ILIT is often grantor-taxed to you or designed to minimize retained ordinary income.

3) Other Legacy Tools That Pair Well

- Dynasty Trust (long-term ILIT variant): For states that allow long trust durations; preserves wealth for multiple generations.
- SLAT (Spousal Lifetime Access Trust): One spouse gifts to a trust benefiting the other; keeps access indirectly while removing assets from the estate.
- Trust Protector: A neutral "referee" empowered to replace trustees, fix drafting glitches, or move the trust if laws change.
- Situs choice: Some states (e.g., SD, NV, DE) offer stronger privacy, creditor protection, and long perpetuities periods. Your attorney can set up the trust there even if you live elsewhere.

- Family Holding LLC: The trust owns the LLC; the LLC owns properties. This streamlines management, adds a liability buffer, and simplifies gifting membership interests.

4) Two-Trust System Together

1. Acquire property inside an LLC.
2. Title the LLC membership interest to your revocable trust.
3. Operate and improve properties; depreciation and step-up benefits stay intact.
4. Fund the irrevocable life insurance trust with life insurance, gifts, or premium financing.
5. Borrow against policy cash values (per trust rules) for education, first homes, or new investments—your family bank.
6. At death, policy proceeds hit the ILIT tax-free, refreshing the family bank; RLT assets transfer to heirs or continuing trusts without probate and with step-up.

This is control today + protection forever.

5) Choosing the Right People

RLT Trustee

- Often you first successor should be organized, calm, and decisive.
- Must be willing to follow your playbook (Family Constitution + trust terms).

ILIT Trustee

- Consider a professional / corporate trustee or a trusted individual plus a corporate co-trustee.
- Must be strong enough to say no to entitled requests.

- Should be familiar with policy management (loans, interest, MEC limits, premium finance covenants).

Advisory circle (non-fiduciary but essential)

- Tax strategist/CPA (not just a form-filler).
- Estate attorney (trust designer and state law navigator).
- Insurance specialist (in force monitoring, funding "to the bubble," non-MEC design).
- Real estate counsel (deeds, entity compliance).

Pro move: add a Trust Protector with limited powers (replace trustees, change situs, approve decanting) to future-proof the plan.

6) Funding & Titling Checklist

Revocable Trust

- Deed each property from your name/old entity to the LLC (if not already).
- Assign LLC membership interests to the RLT.
- Retitle personal accounts (or name the trust as pay-on-death where appropriate).
- Update beneficiary designations (IRAs/401(k)s typically name individuals or conduit trusts—coordinate with your attorney).
- Execute a pour-over will.
- Update homeowner/landlord insurance to match new titling.

Irrevocable Trust

- Trust applies for its own EIN.
- Policies issued to the ILIT as owner and beneficiary.

- If transferring an existing policy, watch for a three-year lookback (estate inclusion risk).
- Document gifts and Crummey notices.
- For premium finance: loan docs, collateral schedule, interest budget, exit plan.

If it isn't titled correctly, it isn't protected.

7) Taxes

What Changes, What Doesn't

- **Income tax (RLT):** No change during life; you report all income / expenses.
- **Income tax (ILIT):** Designed to minimize trust-level income (grantor features or limited retained income).
- **Estate/Gift tax:** Thresholds move—build flexibility. The ILIT's purpose is to keep life insurance outside your taxable estate; the RLT does not remove assets from your estate (which is exactly why you get the step-up).
- **Basis step-up:** Generally, yes in RLT; generally, no in ILIT (unless intentionally pulled into estate via powers, which trades protection for basis—case-by-case planning).
- **MEC rules:** Overfund too fast and you lose tax advantages on policy loans. Fund to the bubble, not past it.

(Exact exemption amounts change. Have your attorney or CPA confirm current figures when you finalize.)

8) Common Mistakes (and How to Avoid Them)

1. Creating a trust…then never funding it. (Fix: run a funding audit with your attorney.)
2. Putting rentals in your own name. (Fix: LLC + RLT ownership.)
3. Owning life insurance personally. (Estate inclusion; Fix: ILIT owns it.)
4. No successor plan. (Fix: name layered backups + trust protector.)
5. No paperwork for gifts/Crummey notices. (Fix: calendar and document.)
6. Trust without rules. (Fix: pair with your Family Constitution for behavior + eligibility.)
7. Ignoring in-force policy management. (Fix: annual review of charges, caps, loan balances, MEC testing.)
8. Wrong situs. (Fix: seat in a trust-friendly state when beneficial.)

9) Integrating With Your Family Constitution

- **Eligibility:** Tie access to work ethic, education, and financial literacy milestones.
- **Loans:** Require proposals, mentorship, and approval by a Family Council; unpaid amounts reduce future inheritances.
- **Philanthropy:** Hard-code annual giving targets and a process for selecting causes.
- **Meetings:** Annual Family Retreat (your "board meeting") to review assets, performance, and next-gen education.

The trust is the legal chassis; the Constitution is the operating manual.

A Simple Example: Your Two-Lane Structure

Lane A (RLT/LLC): You own an eighteen-unit building titled in an LLC; LLC membership interests owned by your RLT. You refinance, improve, and operate efficiently; upon death, heirs get step-up and no probate.

Lane B (ILIT/Legacy): Your ILIT owns $X life insurance (some premium-financed). The trust lends for education/home/business under rules; loans reduce future distributions if unpaid. At death, the proceeds replenish the family bank, and new policies on newborns keep the engine running.

The result is liquidity plus protection plus step-up plus governance. They are all pulling in the same direction.

One-Page Action Plan

1. **Retitle:** Move properties into LLCs; assign LLC interests to your Revocable Trust.
2. **Pour-Over Will** + updated POAs/Health Directives.
3. **Establish ILIT** for life insurance; appoint trustee + trust protector.
4. **Fund to the Bubble:** Set the non-MEC funding schedule; document Crummey notices.
5. **Premium Finance (if used):** lock terms, collateral, exit plan; annual in-force reviews.
6. **Write & Adopt the Family Constitution:** set your annual Family Retreat.
7. **Create a Master Binder (physical + digital):** deeds, operating agreements, trust instruments, insurance, loan docs, Crummey letters, contacts.
8. **Calendar Reviews:** legal, tax, and insurance checkups every year—no exceptions.

• • •

Trusts are not about making things complicated. They're about making your intentions inescapably clear and legally enforceable. Your revocable trust keeps operations smooth and tax-smart today. Your irrevocable legacy trust makes sure what you've built is protected, replenished, and guided tomorrow.

You worked too hard to let a courtroom, a creditor, or a divorce attorney write the ending. Put your hands on the steering wheel and keep the family empire pointed in the right direction now and for generations.

At this point, you've built assets, systems, protection, and purpose. What remains isn't strategy—it's execution. In the final chapter, we remove the last obstacle that stops most people from ever starting: hesitation.

CHAPTER 9
THE FINAL PUSH

I just handed you the roadmap to a brand-new life—not only for you but for your family and generations to come. A life where you don't have to wake up dreading the same routine, punching the same clock, and hoping for a small raise once a year. This isn't about gambling, lottery tickets, or hoping for luck. Real estate is a proven vehicle that—if approached with discipline and consistency—can deliver a life of financial independence and freedom.

So what's stopping you?

EXCUSES OR EXECUTION

The most common barriers I hear are the same ones I told myself at the beginning:

"I don't have enough money."

"I don't have enough time."

"The market is too expensive right now."

"What if I fail?"

Here's the truth: every investor—from small to big—started with these same doubts. The difference between those who succeed and those who stay stuck is execution. You don't need to have it all figured out before you start. You just need to start.

Time and money are never perfectly aligned. They never will be. You'll either find reasons why you can't, or you'll find reasons why you must. The latter mindset is what separates the 1% who build wealth from the 99% who keep spinning their wheels.

People overestimate risk and underestimate time. They fear making a mistake, but they don't fear standing still. Yet standing still is the most expensive mistake of all.

Markets will change.

Interest rates will rise and fall.

Rules will evolve.

None of that invalidates the action. It simply changes *how* the action looks. I've never met a successful investor who felt ready before their first deal. I've met many who waited until they felt safe—and never started. Let's be honest. Fear is the real enemy here. Fear of making a mistake. Fear of losing money. Fear of looking foolish. But here's the irony: doing nothing is often the biggest mistake. Sitting on the sidelines guarantees you zero return, zero growth, and zero change in your circumstances.

Think of fear like a tenant. It only lives in your head if you allow it. Evict it. Replace it with execution, education, and persistence.

BREAKING GENERATIONAL PATTERNS

Most financial outcomes are inherited not through money but through behavior. Maybe nobody in your family ever invested in real estate. Maybe your parents told you to play it safe and stick with a job. That's okay. But understand this: if you don't break that cycle, who will? Your kids and grandkids are watching, learning, and modeling their future after yours. By confronting fear and excuses, you're not just building assets, you're rewriting your family's financial legacy.

We repeat what we see:

- Fear around debt
- Silence around money
- Dependency on institutions

- Short-term thinking

Breaking those patterns requires discomfort.

You may be the first in your family to think this way. The first to buy assets instead of liabilities. The first to talk openly about money with your kids. The first to design systems instead of hoping things work out.

That position can feel lonely, and the first deal will always feel like the hardest. But once you close that first deal, your confidence builds, your skills grow, and your opportunities multiply. Suddenly, realtors call you with properties, banks look at you as a proven borrower, and your own mindset shifts from *Can I do this?* to *What's next?*

It's like pushing a heavy flywheel. At first, it takes everything you have to get it moving. But once momentum builds, the wheel turns faster and faster with less effort. The same is true in real estate. The earlier you start, the sooner momentum compounds.

Readiness is not a feeling. It's a decision. Waiting feels harmless. It isn't. Every year you delay:

- Inflation erodes purchasing power
- Opportunity compounds for others
- Time—the one asset you can't replace—disappears

The tragedy isn't failure. The tragedy is unused potential. You don't need to be perfect. You need to be moving.

THE CHALLENGE

So I challenge you: confront the fear, confront the excuses, and commit to the journey. Whether it's starting small with a duplex, exploring seller financing, or house-hacking your first property, the point is to take that first step.

You've come this far. You now know more than most people will ever take the time to learn. The only question left is: *What are you going to do with it?*

Every generational shift starts with someone willing to be uncomfortable early, so others don't have to struggle later. I see it more and more these days. My daughter's friends are still living at home at twenty-four, working, saving a little, and spending weekends at the beach. It's survival mode disguised as freedom. I even have a tenant who illustrates this perfectly: He's thirty years old, living on the second floor. His godfather lives downstairs and covers his rent in full. He hasn't figured out what he wants to do yet. That isn't support; it's enabling. Life isn't supposed to be easy, and shielding someone from reality only delays their growth.

That's why I call your generation the NINJA generation: **N**o **I**ncome, **N**o **J**ob security, and No **A**ssets. It's not an insult; it's a wake-up call. You've got the drive and the work ethic. What you need now is a new playbook, one that breaks you out of survival mode and into a system for building assets, wealth, and freedom.

FROM SURVIVAL MODE TO FINANCIAL FREEDOM

Right now, your generation is being squeezed out of the traditional American dream. The dream of owning a bigger house than your parents, driving a better car, and taking real vacations feels like a mirage. Just look at the math. In many markets, an average home will cost $700,000 to over $1 million within the next five years. With wages lagging, many young adults will remain long-term renters, not because they're lazy, but because the deck is stacked.

You work hard. You put in eight hours a day (or longer), yet every paycheck seems to evaporate. Rent, taxes, insurance, groceries; it's all survival mode. By the time Friday comes, the cash is gone. This isn't about effort; it's about a system designed to keep you trading hours for dollars forever.

But you *can* flip the script.

FLIP THE SCRIPT

Start by using the very tools the wealthy rely on but rarely talk about. Execute the strategies in this book: buy assets that pay you back, focus on cash-flowing real estate, and—this is critical—use properly structured life insurance as a tax-free generational wealth engine.

A well-designed indexed universal life (IUL) policy can function like your own private bank. You fund it, it grows tax-advantaged, and you can borrow against the cash value tax-free to invest, seize opportunities, or supplement income—all while your heirs inherit the death benefit outside of probate and income taxes. Combine that with disciplined real-estate investing, and you create a flywheel: assets buy more assets, your money compounds while you sleep, and your children inherit not just cash, but a system that keeps compounding for them.

You have a choice. You can stay in society's programming—work, pay bills, hope to retire—or you can build assets that free you decades earlier. You can stay a lifelong renter or become a landlord. You can keep letting taxes eat every raise, or you can leverage tax-advantaged vehicles like real estate and life insurance to build a legacy.

The Tools

- **Acquire Assets Early.** Assets are anything that puts money in your pocket—rental property, a cash-flowing business, or investments that generate income.
- **Leverage Smart Debt.** Use financing for appreciating, income-producing assets, not consumer purchases that lose value.
- **Automate Wealth** build habits—automatic transfers to investment accounts, regular property analysis—that compound quietly over decades.

These strategies are how you escape the paycheck-to-paycheck treadmill and create financial freedom: the state where your assets generate enough income to cover your living expenses, whether you work or not.

A YOUNG INVESTOR WHO BROKE OUT

A friend's son, Mike, was just twenty-three when he bought his first duplex. He didn't wait until he felt ready or had the perfect job. He worked a regular nine-to-five job, saved aggressively for a year, and instead of blowing his tax refund or bonus on vacations or a new car, he used it for a down payment. He moved into one unit and rented out the other. Suddenly, half his living expenses disappeared. Within two years, he repeated the process and bought a triplex.

While his peers were still living at home or paying two thousand dollars a month in rent, Mike's tenants were paying down his mortgages and building equity for him. At twenty-eight, he had six units, positive cash flow, and an asset base that banks respected. His friends laughed at him for not living it up in his twenties. Now he vacations on cash flow, not credit cards.

This is the script-flip in action. It's not about being smarter or luckier. It's about having the courage to take that first step when everyone else is still hesitating.

A NEW MINDSET

The hardest shift isn't technical; it's mental. You must stop thinking like a permanent employee and start thinking like an owner. Owners build systems. They focus on net worth, not job titles. They care about cash flow and cap rates more than corner offices.

Yes, the deck feels stacked. Housing costs are high, and wages lag. But you have one powerful advantage: time. A twenty- or twenty-five-year-old who acts now can let compounding work for decades. Start with a single duplex. Launch a side business. Put every spare dollar to work instead of into lifestyle inflation.

YOUR NEXT MOVE

1. **Educate Yourself.** Financial literacy isn't optional anymore. Learn the basics of real estate analysis, tax strategy, and investing.
2. **Start Small.** Your first asset doesn't have to be huge. A house hack, a cash-flowing rental, or a micro-business can change your trajectory.
3. **Reject the Script.** Stop waiting for raises to save you. Stop assuming a corporate job is security.
4. **Commit.** The first deal is the hardest. After that, momentum—and confidence—build.

You may feel like a NINJA today, but you're not doomed to stay one. With discipline, strategy, and action—leveraging cash-flowing real estate *and* tax-advantaged life-insurance strategies—you can transform from no assets to a generation of owners. Society's programming says work until sixty-seven, then maybe retire. My challenge to you: Break that cycle. Start now. Build assets. Use the same tools the ultra-wealthy use to buy back your freedom and secure your family's legacy.

WHAT FINANCIAL FREEDOM ALLOWS YOU TO DO

One of the areas where I've been able to truly diversify—beyond buying and selling businesses, building a large real estate portfolio, and helped grow one of the largest licensed Article 28 multi-specialty medical group practices in New York for which I sold—is in a field I'm deeply passionate about: stem cell research and regenerative medicine.

I bring the same mindset to this space that I bring to real estate and business. I never ask *"Can this be done?"* or *"How hard will this be?"* I ask one question: How do we solve the problem? That approach led us to a breakthrough that separates what we do from most of the industry.

Our work focuses on using a patient's own cells—a homologous, autologous approach—rather than introducing foreign substances or drug-based interactions. At Advanced Therapeutic Lab here in the US, we've developed a proprietary process that allows us to produce cells in the millions and even billions, where others simply can't. And we do it without enzymes, without collagenase, and without growth factors. That difference matters. It means no drug interaction, no foreign material, and 100% biological acceptance by the body.

That's not theory—it's outcomes.

Some of our largest clients have come from the NFL and Major League Baseball, where performance and recovery matter at the highest level. But that's not what stays with me. What stays with me is watching someone who was partially paralyzed walk again. Or seeing someone who had lost hearing in one ear regain it. Those moments remind you why solving real problems—not just generating revenue—matters.

My financial success—particularly through real estate—gave me the freedom to invest in areas like this. When you're not trapped by paycheck-to-paycheck thinking or dependent on outside capital, you can fund innovation on your own terms. Stem cell therapy is one of those areas where I'm confident the long-term impact will be profound—once innovation is allowed to move forward without being strangled by entrenched interests.

I'll never forget walking into one of the most prestigious medical centers in the country to discuss treatments for neuropathy and multiple sclerosis. Halfway through the meeting, the physician excused everyone from the room except the two of us. He leaned in and said quietly, *"Are you out of your mind? We need to fill these beds. We need these people sick. We can't have this."*

That moment changed how I see healthcare.

It's when you realize how many breakthroughs never reach patients—not because they don't work, but because they disrupt the economics of medicine. We've likely cured cancer a hundred times over. The patents get bought, shelved, and hung on a wall somewhere. Sickness is profitable. Health is disruptive.

This is why financial independence matters.

When your income and assets give you freedom, you're no longer forced to play by broken systems. You can fund innovation. You can challenge the status quo. You can invest not just for returns—but for impact. And that, to me, is what real wealth is ultimately about.

FINAL LETTER TO MY YOUNGER SELF

My Dearest Glenn,

If you are reading this book, then somehow I managed to get this message to you back in time. In your hands is not just a book, but a playbook, one that maps out the journey I've lived, the mistakes I've made, and the wisdom I've earned along the way. It is my gift to you, so that you can step forward with clarity, courage, and confidence, without wasting years stumbling in the dark as I once did.

First, let me be absolutely clear: do not sit idle. Don't just dream, don't just plan, don't just ponder. Take action. The clock is always ticking, and hesitation is the enemy of success. You will never feel ready. You will never have all the answers. But what you will have is the ability to move, to learn, to adapt, and to build. And that is enough.

Don't fear failure. That word doesn't even exist in our family's vocabulary. Failure is not an ending, it is a steppingstone. Every misstep, every setback, every challenge you'll face is not designed to break you but to shape you. If you stumble, get up. If you lose, learn. If you fall behind, sprint harder. That is the formula, and it will serve you for life.

Here's something else I want you to know: your greatest investment will not be in properties or bank accounts. It will be in people. Your wife, Theresa, is not just a partner, but the teammate of a lifetime. Together, you will build not only a family but a legacy. You'll raise three incredible children—Tyler, Jordan, and Ryan—each with their own talents, their own ambitions, and their own role to play in carrying the torch forward. Treasure them. Guide them. Challenge them. They are the reason all of this matters.

Now, let's talk about wealth. Not the kind that sits in a bank, but the kind that creates freedom. Freedom from corporate handcuffs. Freedom from fear of bills. Freedom from the illusion that security comes from a job title. You will learn that real wealth is built through assets—real estate, trusts, and systems that compound over time. Build them early, build them smart, and protect them fiercely.

But wealth without discipline is a curse. You must also build a work ethic so strong that nothing—not holidays, not obstacles, not excuses—can shake it. There will be nights you'll fix water heaters on Christmas Eve. There will be weekends when friends are out partying, and you'll be working on your vision. Do it anyway. Because every sacrifice, every grind, every late night and early morning will eventually stack up into a life you could never have imagined when you first started.

If I could give you one phrase to carry with you always, it would be this: Think generationally. Don't build for today. Don't even build just for yourself. Build for your children, your grandchildren, and the ones who will never meet you but will live better because of you. Put your assets into trusts, structure your estate, protect your family with insurance, and educate them so they never squander what you worked so hard to build. That is how you turn wealth into legacy.

I urge you to take this book and not only read it, but live it. It is your map to freedom, to family, to fulfillment. If you ignore it, if you let fear or doubt hold you back, then one day you will look back with regret. But if you embrace it, if you act with courage and conviction, then one day you'll look at your life with gratitude and awe, knowing you gave your family the most priceless gift: the foundation of generational wealth.

With love, persistence, and unwavering belief in you,

Your Older Self

If you've made it this far, I want to thank you. Whether you are my younger self, my children, my grandchildren, or simply someone who picked up this book in search of answers, know this: the principles I've written here are not theory. They are lived principles tested through decades of persistence and trial.

The road to wealth is not paved with shortcuts or luck. It is paved with discipline, sacrifice, and the courage to think differently. Real estate gave me the tools. Life insurance and trusts gave me the structure. But what truly built my life was persistence, hard work, and the decision to never quit when things got hard.

My hope is that you use these lessons not just to build wealth, but to build freedom for yourself, for your family, and for generations yet to come. May you carry forward the same fire that drove me, and may you pass that fire on, brighter than before.

Remember, wealth fades without wisdom, and money without meaning will always vanish. But when you combine knowledge, discipline, and purpose, you create not just riches, but you create a legacy.

CHAPTER 10
GENERATIONAL WEALTH CHALLENGE RULES

CHALLENGE RULES, OVERVIEW, & LEGAL DETAILS

SECTION 1 – CHALLENGE OVERVIEW

The Generational Wealth Challenge - Presented by The Guide To Wealth, LLC

Build Your First Multi-Family Property — Without Starting From Zero

What if one book could change your family's financial trajectory forever?

Here's how it works - The Generational Wealth Challenge is our way of turning education into action. Through this Challenge, we will award **ten (10) grant prizes**, each valued at **$100,000**, designed to help real people acquire their first **2–4 family investment property** and begin building generational wealth the right way.

The Generational Wealth Challenge is sponsored by **The Guide To Wealth, LLC** ("Sponsor"), located in the United States.

SECTION 2 – GRANT PROGRAM DESCRIPTION

Each Grant Award Includes:

• $70,000 investment grant applied toward the down payment of a 2–4 family residential property

• $7,000 in legal support, including LLC formation, lease templates, and asset protection guidance

• $10,000 in tax strategy planning, including depreciation strategy, rental tax optimization, and long-term structuring

• **$13,000 for** Access to experienced real estate professionals for coaching, deal analysis, and financial strategy guidance

Important:

The $100,000 Grant Award, consisting of down payment assistance, legal support, tax strategy planning, and professional coaching, will be paid directly by The Guide To Wealth, LLC to approved service providers and not to the winner.

Winners are responsible for all applicable federal and state taxes.

How Winners Are Selected:

- One winner is selected for every 100,000 verified books sales across all formats and retailers.
- Winners are chosen randomly
- Each selection will be:
  - Conducted live
  - Streamed publicly
  - Announced on theguidetowealth.com and official social media channels
- Winners must adhere to the participation guidelines further described in the Legal Terms, Conditions and Program Disclosures.
- Selection dates will be posted at least two weeks in advance and posted on the theguidetowealth.com website.

How to Enter:

We created this program to demonstrate that financial education should lead to opportunity—not just information. By turning knowledge into action, this initiative helps individuals take their first step toward owning an income-producing asset and building long-term financial stability.

Why We're Doing This

The goal of this Challenge isn't hype — it's impact.

Most people are never taught how to:

- Buy income-producing assets
- Use tax strategy legally
- Protect what they build
- Create wealth that lasts beyond one generation

NO PURCHASE NECESSARY TO ENTER OR WIN. A PURCHASE OR PAYMENT OF ANY KIND WILL NOT INCREASE YOUR CHANCES OF WINNING.

This Challenge exists to give real people a real starting point—not cash prizes, but a system.

If you purchase *The Generational Wealth and Real Estate Playbook,* you may earn entry to the give-away as follows:

1. Purchase the book (any format)
2. Inside the book, locate the hidden catch phrase
   - The catch phrase is two words
   - Clues are hidden within the illustrations/graphics
3. Visit theguidetowealth.com
4. Submit:
   - The catch phrase
   - Provide a Copy of Proof of purchase of the book with your name and date on the receipt.

Submit proof of purchase = **1 entry**

Correctly identify the catch phrase = **4 additional entries**

Maximum entries from book participation: five (5).

Optional Bonus Entries = Earn 10 additional entries. Optional Bonus Entries are available only after a valid book purchase entry has been submitted.

You may earn additional give-away entries by:

Posting an Instagram story or post sharing three things you liked about the book & tag at least 5 people about the book.

Liking the guidetowealth Instagram, TikTok & Facebook official account

Using both hashtags:

#TheGenerationalWealthandRealEstatePlaybook

#theguidetowealth

IMPORTANT NOTES

- Winners must meet eligibility requirements and complete verification
- Failure to respond or comply may result in forfeiture
- The promotion is open to U.S. residents **except where prohibited by law.**
- Sponsor reserves the right to restrict participation in jurisdictions requiring registration or bonding.
- This promotion is in no way sponsored, endorsed, administered by, or associated with Instagram, Facebook, TikTok, Amazon, or any other third-party platform.
- Limit one (1) book purchase entry per person and one (1) mail-in entry per person per drawing period.
- Winners must respond within **7 days of notification** or an alternate winner may be selected.

Option 2: Free Mail-In Entry (No Purchase Required)

You may enter the give-away without buying the book by mailing a postcard.

Mail-In Entry Instructions

Send a handwritten 3" x 5" postcard including:

- Full Name
- Mailing Address
- Email Address
- Phone Number
- The statement: "I am entering the Generational Wealth Challenge."

Mail to:

The Guide to Wealth, LLC

Generational Wealth Challenge

PO Box 13

Ringwood, NJ 07456

Optional Bonus Entries are available only after a valid book purchase entry has been submitted.

- Postcard must be postmarked by the published deadline
- A purchase will not increase your odds of winning.
- Entries become the property of the Sponsor and will not be returned.

Learn More

Full Official Rules, entry deadlines, and live drawing dates are available at: **theguidetowealth.com**

SECTION 3 – OFFICIAL RULES

Generational Wealth Grant Program - Turning Financial Education Into Real Opportunity

Grant Award Package

Each selected Fellow receives a structured wealth-building package designed to support responsible asset ownership and long-term financial success.

Who the Grant Is Designed To Help

The Generational Wealth Grant Program prioritizes individuals who can benefit from financial education and structured support in building long-term economic stability. You must be at least 18 years or older.

Mission of the Program

The purpose of the Generational Wealth Grant Program is to help individuals gain access to the same financial strategies that have historically helped families build lasting wealth.

These include:

- Real estate ownership
- Strategic tax planning
- Asset protection
- Responsible financial decision-making

By combining education, mentorship, and structured financial support, the program aims to help participants create long-term financial stability that can benefit future generations.

Why This Matters

For too long, financial knowledge has been unevenly distributed. This Program exists to help change that. Because building wealth should not depend on where you started. It should depend on what you are willing to learn. Participation in the Program constitutes full acceptance of the terms outlined below. This Program is not intended to constitute investment advice, financial guarantees, or a promise of financial success.

Program Duration

The Generational Wealth Grant Program shall remain active until the earliest occurrence of one of the following events:

1. A total of 1,000,000 copies of *The Generational Wealth and Real Estate Playbook* have been sold and ten (10) grants of $100,000 each have been awarded, or
2. Two (2) years have elapsed from the official publication date of the book, whichever occurs first.

During the Program period, grants will be awarded proportionally based on verified book distribution milestones.

Examples:

- 100,000 books sold → 1 grant awarded
- 200,000 books sold → 2 grants awarded
- 300,000 books sold → 3 grants awarded

If fewer than 1,000,000 books are sold within the two-year Program period, the number of grants awarded will correspond proportionally to the number of books sold. Under no circumstances shall The Guide to Wealth, LLC be obligated to award more than ten (10) grants.

ELIGIBILITY

The Challenge is open to legal residents of the United States, excluding residents of New York, Florida, and Rhode Island, who are 18 years of age or older at the time of entry. Void where prohibited by law.

Not eligible:

- Employees, officers, directors, of the Guide To Wealth, LLC
- Immediate family members (spouse, parents, children) of the Sponsor
- Any individual prohibited by law from receiving prizes of this nature
- Entrants must provide truthful and accurate information when submitting entries.

Other Conditions:

No cash alternative is available.

- All funds are paid directly by The Guide to Wealth, LLC to approved professionals, vendors, or service providers as selected for the winner by The Guide to Wealth, LLC.
- Funds may not be reassigned, transferred, or substituted.
- Winners are solely responsible for all federal, state, and local taxes.
- Failure to participate in required onboarding or planning sessions may result in forfeiture.

ODDS OF WINNING

Odds depend on the total number of eligible entries received.

GENERAL CONDITIONS

The Sponsor reserves the right to:

- Verify eligibility
- Disqualify entries that are incomplete, inaccurate, or fraudulent
- Modify or cancel the Challenge if fraud, technical failure, or legal issues arise

By entering, participants agree to be bound by these Official Rules and Sponsor decisions, which are final.

PUBLICITY RELEASE

Except where prohibited by law, winners grant permission for the Sponsor to use their name, likeness, and story for promotional purposes without additional compensation or release.

LIMITATION OF LIABILITY

The Sponsor is not responsible for:

- Lost, late, or misdirected entries
- Technical failures
- Platform outages
- Errors in prize fulfillment due to circumstances beyond reasonable control

WINNERS LIST

A list of winners will be posted on **theguidetowealth.com** after each drawing.

FINAL NOTE

This Challenge is designed to educate, empower, and deploy capital responsibly—not to promote gambling or chance-based financial decisions.

SECTION 4 – LEGAL TERMS & DISCLOSURES

No Guarantee of Investment Performance

The Program provides financial education and structured support. Neither the book nor The Guide to Wealth, LLC guarantees:

- Real estate investment returns
- Property appreciation
- Rental income
- Financial outcomes

Recipients acknowledge that real estate investments involve risk and that The guide to Wealth, LLC shall not be responsible for any financial losses associated with property ownership or investment decisions.

Tax Responsibility

Recipients are solely responsible for any federal, state, or local taxes associated with grants or services received through the Program.

The Guide to Wealth, LLC may issue appropriate tax documentation, including but not limited to IRS Form 1099, reflecting the fair market value of services provided.

Recipients agree to indemnify and hold The Guide to Wealth, LLC, The Book – The Generational Wealth and Real Estate Playbook and its Publisher harmless from any tax liability associated with the grant. The fair market value of services provided through the Grant may be reported to the recipient and the Internal Revenue Service on Form 1099 or other applicable tax documentation.

Limitation of Liability

To the fullest extent permitted by law, The Guide to Wealth, LLC, The Book – The Generational Wealth and Real Estate Playbook and its

Publisher, officers, employees, volunteers, affiliates, advisors, and partners shall not be liable for any:

- Financial losses
- Investment losses
- Property disputes
- Legal or tax issues
- Personal damages or claims arising from participation in the Program.

Participants assume all risks associated with property ownership, financing decisions, and investment activities.

PROGRAM MODIFICATION OR TERMINATION

The Guide to Wealth, LLC, The Book – The Generational Wealth and Real Estate Playbook reserves the right, at its sole discretion, to modify, suspend, or terminate the Program if circumstances arise that could compromise the integrity, legality, or feasibility of the Program.

Such circumstances may include, but are not limited to:

- Legal or regulatory requirements
- Fraud or abuse
- Insufficient participation
- Financial limitations
- Force majeure events

In the event of termination, The Guide to Wealth, LLC, The Book – The Generational Wealth and Real Estate Playbook and its Publisher shall have no obligation beyond awards already granted.

PARTICIPANT RELEASE

By applying to or participating in the Program, participants release and hold harmless The Guide to Wealth, LLC, The Book – The Generational Wealth and Real Estate Playbook and its Publisher and its affiliates from any and all liability, claims, damages, or legal actions arising from participation in the Program or use of Grant resources.

Publisher and Third-Party Indemnification

The author, Glenn Polansky, and The Guide to Wealth, LLC, The Book – The Generational Wealth and Real Estate Playbook agree to indemnify, defend, and hold harmless the book's publisher, distributors, retailers, and all affiliated entities, including but not limited to Amazon, booksellers, and digital platforms, from any claims, liabilities, damages, or expenses arising from or related to the Generational Wealth Grant Program.

The publisher and all book distribution partners are not responsible for administering, managing, or fulfilling the Program and bear no liability related to its operation. The publisher's involvement is limited solely to **the publication and distribution** of the book.

Governing Law

These terms shall be governed by and construed in accordance with the laws of the United States and the state of NJ without regard to conflict-of-law principles.

Acceptance of Terms

Participation in the Generational Wealth Grant Program constitutes full acceptance of these terms and conditions. Applicants acknowledge that they have read, understood, and agree to comply with the Program rules and legal disclosures.

No Investment Advice

The content contained in *The Generational Wealth and Real Estate Playbook*, as well as any materials provided through the Generational Wealth Grant Program, is intended solely for educational and informational purposes. Nothing contained in the book, on the website, or within the Program should be interpreted as investment advice, financial advice, legal advice, tax advice, or real estate brokerage services. Readers and participants are strongly encouraged to consult with qualified licensed professionals, including financial advisors, attorneys, accountants, and real estate professionals, before making any financial or investment decisions.

Neither Glenn Polansky, The Guide to Wealth, LLC, The Book – The Generational Wealth and Real Estate Playbook and its Publisher acts as an investment advisor, broker, financial planner, attorney, accountant, or licensed professional in connection with the Program unless explicitly stated otherwise.

No Reliance Clause

By participating in the Program or reading the book, individuals acknowledge that they are not relying solely on any statements, examples, projections, or educational materials provided by the author when making financial or investment decisions. All financial decisions, including real estate acquisitions, financing arrangements, and tax strategies, remain the sole responsibility of the participant. Participants understand that past results or examples referenced in the book or Program do not guarantee future outcomes.

Educational Purpose Disclaimer

The Program and related materials are designed to provide general educational information about real estate ownership, tax planning concepts, and financial literacy. Any examples of financial outcomes, investment strategies, or property acquisitions are illustrative only and should not be interpreted as guarantees or promises of financial success. Real estate investing involves risk, including the risk of loss of capital, market fluctuations, tenant vacancy, interest rate changes, property maintenance expenses, and economic conditions.

No Agency Relationship

Participation in the Generational Wealth Grant Program does not create any partnership, joint venture, agency, fiduciary relationship, or advisory relationship between the participant and The Guide to Wealth, LLC, The Book – The Generational Wealth and Real Estate Playbook and its Publisher or Glenn Polansky. Participants remain fully responsible for their own financial, legal, and investment decisions.

Third-Party Service Providers

Legal, tax, and professional services associated with Grant awards may be provided by independent third-party professionals selected or approved by The Guide to Wealth, LLC. The Guide to Wealth, LLC, The Book – The Generational Wealth and Real Estate Playbook and its Publisher and the author do not control the actions of these professionals and make no representations or warranties regarding their services. Participants agree that any disputes related to such services must be resolved directly with the service provider.

Publisher Protection and Indemnification

The author, Glenn Polansky, The Guide to Wealth, LLC, The Book – The Generational Wealth and Real Estate Playbook and its Publisher agree to indemnify, defend, and hold harmless the publisher, distributors, booksellers, retailers, and digital platforms associated with the book from any claims, damages, liabilities, or expenses arising from the Generational Wealth Grant Program. The publisher and distribution partners have no responsibility for administering, managing, or fulfilling the Grant Program, and shall bear no liability related to the Program. All promotional activities, awards, and Program administration are the sole responsibility of The Guide to Wealth, LLC

Website and Online Platform Disclaimer

The website, **theguidetowealth.com**, and related digital platforms are provided for informational purposes only. The Guide to Wealth, LLC, The Book – The Generational Wealth and Real Estate Playbook and its Publisher does not guarantee that website access will be uninterrupted, error-free, or free of technical issues. The Guide to Wealth, LLC, The Book – The Generational Wealth and Real Estate Playbook and its Publisher shall not be responsible for lost submissions, technical failures, or interruptions in online services. As well as not responsible for lost, incomplete, illegible, delayed, or misdirected entries, whether submitted electronically or by mail.

Entire Agreement

These legal terms and disclosures constitute the entire agreement governing participation in the Generational Wealth Grant Program and supersede any prior communications or representations regarding the Program.

Amendments

The Guide to Wealth, LLC, The Book – The Generational Wealth and Real Estate Playbook reserves the right to update or amend these terms at any time in order to comply with legal requirements, improve program administration, or address unforeseen circumstances.

Updated terms will be posted on **theguidetowealth.com**.

Severability

If any provision of these terms is determined to be invalid or unenforceable under applicable law, the remaining provisions shall continue in full force and effect.

Fraud Protection Clause:

The Guide to Wealth, LLC, The Book – The Generational Wealth and Real Estate Playbook reserves the right to disqualify any participant suspected of tampering with the entry process, submitting fraudulent information, attempting to obtain multiple entries through deceptive means, or otherwise violating the spirit of the program.

EPILOGUE: THE NEXT CHAPTER IS YOURS

As I finish these pages, I think back to the boy delivering newspapers at dawn, sprinting to pick up tennis balls, and dreaming of something bigger. I think of the man who worked late nights fixing boilers, studying loan documents, and patching drywall while others slept. And I think of the father and husband who built not only wealth, but a family, a legacy, and a future.

This book has been my roadmap, my lessons learned, my battle scars, and my victories. But now, it no longer belongs to me; it belongs to you.

The truth is simple: no one is coming to save you. Not your job, not the government, not the lottery. Freedom is built, not handed out. And you build it through assets, discipline, and persistence. You build it by showing up when others quit, by thinking generationally when others think only of today, and by daring to take risks when others stay frozen in fear.

You now know the secrets the wealthy have used for generations—trusts, life insurance, leverage, real estate, and above all, mindset. But knowledge alone is not power. Applied knowledge is power. If you close this book and do nothing, then nothing changes. If you take even one step—make one call, run one number, attend one showing—then you have shifted your future.

My greatest hope is that when you look back years from now, you'll see this book not as something you read but as something you lived. That you'll have stories of your own—of the deals you fought for, the setbacks you overcame, the assets you built, and the legacy you created.

When that day comes, pass it on. Teach your children. Teach their children. Share the playbook, but also share the grit, the work ethic, and the courage to keep building. Because true wealth is not just money—it's wisdom, discipline, and legacy.

The next chapter is not mine to write. It's yours. Pick up the pen and make it extraordinary. So go, take the first step. Build, protect, and grow. Make your life extraordinary, and may generations yet unborn thank you for the courage you showed today.

You don't need to go back in time to change your future.

You just need to act today.

Turn the page.

THE NEXT CHAPTER IS YOURS

TAKE THE NEXT STEP WITH THE REAL ESTATE INVESTOR SYSTEM

Reading this book will give you the mindset, principles, and strategies needed to build wealth through real estate. But success in real estate does not come from knowledge alone. It comes from having the right systems, the right documents, and the right tools in place from the beginning.

One of the biggest mistakes new and growing investors make is trying to piece everything together on their own. They use outdated forms, incomplete leases, weak screening processes, or rough deal calculations that fail to capture the true numbers. Those early mistakes can cost you thousands of dollars, create unnecessary stress, and slow down your growth.

That is exactly why I created the **Real Estate Investor System**, available through **theguidetowealth.com**.

This system is designed to help you get started the right way by giving you practical, real-world tools you can begin using immediately in your business. Instead of guessing, reinventing the wheel, or learning through expensive trial and error, you will have access to the same type of structured resources serious investors rely on to analyze opportunities, protect their properties, and run their operations more professionally.

Inside this package, you will receive:

- **My Deal Analyzer**
- **My Lease Agreements**
- **My Rental Application**
- **My Check-In Forms**
- **My Check-Out Forms**
- **Property Management Plans and Guidelines**

Each of these tools serves a specific purpose.

The **Deal Analyzer** helps you evaluate opportunities more clearly so you can make smarter investment decisions and avoid overpaying for a property or underestimating your costs.

The **Lease Agreements** help establish clear expectations and stronger protection by putting the right structure in place between you and your tenants from day one.

The **Rental Application** helps you create a more professional tenant screening process so you can reduce risk and make better decisions before a tenant ever moves in.

The **Check-In and Check-Out Forms** help document property condition, reduce disputes, and create accountability at move-in and move-out.

The **Property Management Plans and Guidelines** help you operate more efficiently, stay organized, and create consistency in the way your rentals are managed.

Taken together, this package is meant to help you avoid common mistakes, save time, reduce confusion, and build your rental business on a stronger foundation. Whether you are buying your first investment property or expanding an existing portfolio, having the right tools can make the difference between operating reactively and operating with confidence.

Too many investors start with enthusiasm but without structure. They learn lessons only after dealing with tenant issues, paperwork problems, missed details, or bad numbers on a deal. My goal is to help you avoid those unnecessary mistakes by giving you systems that can put you on the right path from the start.

As you have seen throughout this book, my journey in real estate was not built without mistakes. Many of the lessons I share came from real-world challenges, costly missteps, and years of learning what works and what does not. The system I offer today is the result of more than 30 years of hands-on experience buying properties, managing tenants, solving problems, and continually refining every part of the process. I have amended, improved, and strengthened these tools over time with one goal in mind: to create a system that helps investors avoid common pitfalls and get off to the right start. What you are receiving is not a collection of generic forms, but a practical, field-tested system developed by someone who has lived this business for decades. For readers who have taken in the lessons of this book and are ready to move from understanding to action, this package is designed to help you do so with greater clarity, structure, and confidence.

You can access the full **Real Estate Investor System** at: **theguidetowealth.com**

If you are serious about building wealth through real estate, this package will help you move forward with greater clarity, better organization, and a more professional approach.

ABOUT THE AUTHOR

Glenn Polansky is a real estate investor, entrepreneur, and business executive with more than three decades of experience building, operating, and scaling complex organizations across real estate, healthcare, and finance.

Over the last 30 years, Glenn has personally built and managed a substantial multi-family real estate portfolio, focusing on long-term cash flow, tax efficiency, asset protection, and generational wealth strategies. His hands-on experience spans acquisitions, financing, property operations, refinancing, and portfolio scaling — giving him a real-world perspective rarely found in traditional personal finance books.

Professionally, Glenn has served as Chief Executive Officer, President, and senior executive for several large healthcare organizations, including national insurance companies, medical groups, and startup ventures. Throughout his career, he has overseen hundreds of millions of dollars in revenue, led large operational teams, and worked directly with federal and state regulators, financial institutions, and legal teams — experience that deeply shaped his understanding of risk management, leverage, and strategic planning.

Glenn holds a Master's Degree in Health Administration from the **University of Southern California** and a Bachelor's Degree from **Rutgers University**. Earlier in life, he was a professional tennis player, an experience that helped instill the discipline, competitiveness, and long-term mindset that continues to guide his investing philosophy today.

Driven by a passion for financial literacy, Glenn wrote *The Generational Wealth & Real Estate Playbook* to give younger generations the roadmap he wishes he had at 20 — one built on real estate, tax strategy, leverage, asset protection, and legacy planning. His mission is simple: help families stop trading time for money and start building systems that create freedom for generations.

Glenn lives in New Jersey with his wife, Theresa, and their three children, Tyler, Jordan & Ryan, where family, education, and legacy remain at the center of everything he builds.

BACK COVER COPY

The Generational Wealth and Real Estate Playbook is your roadmap to building wealth that doesn't just last — it *lives on*.

Most people work hard their entire lives, yet never break free financially. They earn more, save more, and still feel behind. The problem isn't effort — it's education. No one teaches you how money really works, how the wealthy structure their assets, or how to protect what you build from taxes, lawsuits, and time itself.

In this book, real estate investor and wealth strategist **Glenn Polansky** shares the exact playbook he spent over 30 years learning through real-world experience — not theory, not hype, and not shortcuts.

This is a **practical guide built on four core pillars**:

• **Generational Wealth** — building systems, not just assets, so your family doesn't start over every generation

• **Real Estate** — using cash-flowing property as the engine for long-term wealth

• **Tax Savings Strategies** — legally minimizing taxes through proven structures and planning

• **Asset Protection** — shielding what you build from lawsuits, creditors, divorce, and unnecessary loss

You'll learn how to think like an owner instead of an employee, how to use leverage responsibly, how to turn equity into opportunity, and how to create a financial structure that continues working long after you're gone.

This isn't a book about getting rich quickly.

It's about getting smart early.

Whether you're just starting out, raising kids, or thinking about your legacy, this playbook gives you the tools, mindset, and strategy to stop reacting financially — and start building intentionally.

Because wealth isn't about what you leave behind.

It's about what you leave *in place.*

www.ingramcontent.com/pod-product-compliance
Lightning Source LLC
LaVergne TN
LVHW100302210926
848480LV00003B/998